Opaque References to the Baltic Sea

Opaque References to the Baltic Sea

Matt Coulee

Opaque References to the Baltic Sea
Copyright © 2013 by Matt Coulee
All rights reserved.

Cover designed by Janie Christiansen & Matt Coulee
Copyright © 2013 by Janie Christiansen & Matt Coulee
All rights reserved.

Published in the United States by Matt Coulee

OpaqueReferences@gmail.com

ISBN 978-0-9910177-3-7 (pbk.)
ISBN 978-0-9910177-1-3 (Kindle)
ISBN 978-0-9910177-2-0 (ePub)

To JMC and PMC,
For helping and inspiring me.

Preface

The following is a journal I kept while traveling abroad. It is copied nearly verbatim except for the alteration of names and minor editing for coherence and literary aesthetic. Each section generally relates to a change in date, place, or subject matter.

"I need you to read this—it's deep and personal and tragic."

{1}

As they hand out famous newspapers I've never heard of, every instruction is repeated in a language I can't understand.

Even the standard pretzels taste different, better, dipped in butter or something.

A bald man of uncertain ethnicity frowns and barely acknowledges my existence as he stands to let me sit next to him.

I didn't get my preferred window or even an aisle, but by some miracle the middle seat next to me is empty.

A strange odor fills the cabin. It isn't necessarily bad, just out of place, like someone snuck a wet dog onboard.

With a giant heave and lurch, our A330 barrels down the runway, jet engines roaring. Soon we're airborne, my fate entirely in the hands of the pilot and Airbus engineering.

Anticipating sleep, I had taken out my contacts prior to takeoff.

My meticulous packing is already paying dividends, along with my new travel bag, although I failed to bring tape, and now my new pocket notebook is beginning to fall apart. Perhaps I should've gotten the kind with spirals at the top.

***

Having just seen The National in concert at Merriweather, I couldn't resist listening to "England" upon landing in London.

Before I could transfer planes to Zurich where I was meeting my buddy Justin, Heathrow made me go through security again. I wasn't prepared for this, and I had to step out of line to organize my liquids. When I finally reentered, I laid my two large contact solution bottles on the conveyor belt and informed the security officer, "This is medical."

He looked at me with a confused expression and replied, "Do you have a medical prescription?"

"No."

"Then you can't take it."

"But it's not open," I said calmly.

Somehow talking my way into an exception if I transferred the solution to smaller clear containers, they temporarily let me through security, so I could go to a store called Boots to buy some empty bottles. They were out of the 100 mL, so I had to buy a bunch of 50 mL.

"Hurry, fill it up. Wait, not here. Over there," he said, pointing to a bench. Pacing, "Hurry." Finally, "Just go."

And I left with my original large bottles. I figured his boss had shown up.

From then on, every person who looked like they were in a hurry, every time there was an announcement over the loud speaker, I thought they were after me. I partially expected security to be waiting at my gate.

London is fascinatingly diverse. The same types of individuals that many people would be freaked out to see getting on a plane are running security. Languages abound, and accents combine with skin tones in a way most Americans would never imagine.

{2}

I didn't eat the entire time I was in Zurich, over twenty hours.

On the train out of town, a Coke cost 5.30 Swiss francs, or nearly $6, and so did water.

Justin and I settled into a "quiet" room where we discussed the possibilities of our immediate travel plans and the equity of the US tax code.

<u>Top Places to Visit/Things to Do:</u>
1. Amsterdam
2. Prague
3. Budapest
4. Oktoberfest

"The European Moon"

The European Moon shines down on my train
and I reflect on that same moon
shining on the continent
for all the centuries before.
Copernicus, Newton, Da Vinci.

All the sleeping armies
looking up at that moon,
the night before battle.
In the woods with clubs,
then swords,
to the waiting muskets,
and finally, the trenches.

That European Moon has seen so much
and so many have looked to her for guidance,
in wonderment,
as I do now,
passing by another old city
in my random railway car.

{3}

We're on the outskirts of Amsterdam, completely unaware of what the night may hold.

After walking the red-light district, we sat down at a bar and watched three girls across the street that were trying to lure customers to their windows. I took some notes on their activity:

- A guy chooses the middle girl and disappears behind a curtain. He went in at 2:04 a.m. and left at 2:12.

- A couple went into a room with the third girl: 2:18 a.m.–

- A second patron visits the middle girl: 2:19–2:28.

- All the passersby ignore the first girl.

- We waited for the couple to return but reluctantly gave up when the bar was closing.

{4}

On a night train from Amsterdam to Copenhagen, a guy from Brazil told me that the US invasion of Iraq was optional. I told him I couldn't disagree.

When we finally made it to a hostel in Copenhagen, I slept with only a sheet because I didn't want to hassle with the bedding. That was a mistake.

We're running out of clothes. I've worn the same socks four days in a row and the same jeans since I first got on the plane in DC.

Our stuff is everywhere. I awake from a fitful night sleep to find maps strewn about the floor—city maps, whole continent maps—always wondering where to go next.

No matter who you're traveling with—it could be Mother Teresa—at times, you will hate them. Mostly it will be misunderstandings mixed with hunger and lack of sleep. On the road though, you have no choice but to talk it out because you got four weeks left together and nowhere to go.

***

Justin is chain-smoking, leaning away from the high winds to expertly light a cigarette. After we went into the city, he ran back to the hostel for another lighter.

I hit on a girl at the bar. "I don't speak English," she told me in perfect English.

Later we walked to Christiania where several Russian-looking guys stood around tables full of pot that had names like Cali Haze and Super Silver Haze.

A teenager sat next to us at a picnic table and was somehow able to roll a joint in the wind. He said he came there daily, so I asked his favorite thing to smoke, and he told me Kashmir.

Soon I was roaming the streets like a junkie looking for Kashmir, going from table to table until I found it at the last one.

Two to three hits and we were done for over an hour.

Then when we tried to light up again, I spilled it on the ground as I leaned forward to get out of the wind.

***

I had a personal epiphany at a Danish museum: religion allows leaders to control the population and to explain the unknown. This was especially important in the old days.

A Danish band called Nephew is awesome.

{5}

<u>Potential Itinerary:</u>

Wednesday the 14th
Copenhagen to Stockholm
Eurail—day 3.

Friday 16th arriving Saturday 17th
Stockholm to Helsinki
60 euros each by ferry or go to Turku for 22 each & use rail pass.

Helsinki to Tallinn
28 euros each for ferry, 2 p.m. departure.

Wednesday the 21st
Tallinn to Warsaw
$142 for a flight.

{6}

In Stockholm, we watched a bird kill another bird. Justin tried to stop it, but he was too late. At first we thought they were fucking, but really one was killing the other.

While waiting for a bus at the port, some people gave us free beers before getting on a cruise ship. The alcohol hit us fast since we'd hardly eaten all day. We're paying for an expensive buffet tomorrow on the ferry to Helsinki.

We could've gotten a discount on a different cruise line, but we didn't want to walk back across town, so we went with the Viking Line instead. We'll see if that works out.

When we get to Helsinki, we're going to visit an old friend of mine, Reko. Well, actually he's not really an old friend—I partied with him one night three years ago. He says he has a place for us to stay.

The Swedish metro was pretty easy to use.

{7}

<u>Meeting Reko:</u>
10:30–11:00 a.m. on the square, Senaatintori of the main cathedral, *tuomiokirkko*.
Biggest white church in the center.
Market square.
Should see from ship.
Big statue in middle of square.

{8}

Maybe I'm no longer running. Has the need to flee finally vanished? If so, is it because I'm better emotionally or just older?

I love the sound of children playing in foreign voices. I don't know what they're saying, but it always sounds so beautiful.

I may take some pictures of Helsinki architecture and post them to Facebook. Possibly the only pics I'll post.

It is disappointing that English is so well-known everywhere. Visiting Scandinavia is practically like visiting a US state in that regard.

I packed light, but I'm certain I could've packed less.

It's so nice to have a solitary moment on this whirlwind trip, sitting on a balcony in Helsinki, writing down thoughts.

On the ferry, Justin met a beautiful Finnish woman who was traveling with a pit bull. While he was talking to her, I introduced myself to a cute girl that worked for the cruise line. Since I don't have cell phone service in Europe, I gave her my email.

Europeans seem much more open and community oriented with their possessions. A girl we talked to in Copenhagen said she let homeless people use her apartment when she was out of town, and now we're staying at Reko's father's flat at the end of the metro line with no problem.

It feels good to have a brief reprieve from the road—to charge devices, collect thoughts, and wash clothes.

I'd really like to take my family to live in Spain, maybe when my future kids are two and four.

I love women. My wife, Shelly, is so great, but is she enough?

I'm kind of becoming a citizen of the world. I travel, come and go. I see people, mostly on trips.

How many more of these will Justin and I do? Is this the last one? Asia? Small cities? South America?

My face feels older. Something seems to have changed. Does it show? Is this the last hurrah?

{9}

I have to find a way to make money that allows me to be free. Writer? Stocks? Blog? Music? Three months on, three months off.

I need to try and keep November, December, and January clear for my work. Do I go back and finish the book I've been working on? I must. It's the key to living the exact kind of life I want.

I feel like I'm finally in control of my life. I can make money when I need to. And make conscious choices. I need to be very careful of taking on new debt, especially for possessions.

I'm surprised at the number of black people in Europe.

There is no place else I'd rather be right now. Lately I get the near overwhelming sense I'm doing exactly what I should; I'm exactly where I ought to be. Although I don't believe in any sort of predetermination, so it probably just relates to some kind of internal fulfillment.

I want to stay in a hotel room for a week with a random girl, or any girl, and fuck every way possible.

{10}

Everyone was putting their trash in wastebaskets when we were in Sweden. We're in Finland one day, and a guy throws a can onto the park ground like it's nothing.

Monday—St. Petersburg
Thursday—Tallinn

{11}

I thought I had found peace, no longer needing to run, but I think I was just tired. The need has returned, a boiling angst to move on, to head to the next city. To escape, flee to fill the void inside me, even if only with exhaustion and learning the road.

I came home at 5 a.m. from a night of heavy drinking to find out in an email from Shelly that my grandmother had died. I felt almost nothing, and Justin and I laughed when I told him later that morning. Not because we didn't care, but rather because we were still drunk and wondering what else could happen on this trip.

I hadn't seen her for six years, and I feel kind of bad about that. She was in a home, and what could I do?

"I'm sorry to have to do this over email, but I just got a message from your sister that said your grandmother passed away today around 1:30 p.m. She doesn't know anything else at the moment but asked me to let you know. I will keep you updated as I find out more information."

"Are you fuckin' serious?"

"I'm sorry, I haven't heard anything else from your family. I will let you know when I know more."

***

My friend Reko kept buying us drinks last night. One of the drinks was mixed with cough syrup or something, and we felt really weird all day on Sunday, so we never left his father's apartment.

Justin found a scarf at the last bar we went to and is going to give it to the Finnish girl he met on the ferry when he visits her in Kouvola on Monday.

{12}

11:32 a.m.
Hi Allan [Allan is the pseudonym I was using on the trip],

It's the girl from the ship :) How long are you staying in Helsinki for?

I'm quite busy atm, I'm going to my hometown at the end of the week, but we could meet up on Wednesday if that's good for you? :)

Mari

2:10 p.m.
Good to hear from you!

I'm not sure if I will be able to meet on Wednesday because we might be going to Tallinn tomorrow.

I can definitely hang out today though. Will you have any time?

Or I could maybe meet you somewhere on Saturday or Sunday. I can pretty much go anywhere.

I'm at the city center right now, but I'm staying at the end of the metro.

Allan

2:50 p.m.
Okay, well I'll be up north in the weekend, but I do have some time over now in the afternoon. So we could grab a cup of coffee. What do you say about meeting outside Stockmann at 4?

3:21 p.m.
Sounds great! See you there.

{13}

We fit together like perfect puzzle pieces. An empty bottle of red wine sits on the table surrounded by chocolate wrappers. An open window lets in the sounds from the street below, people rushing to work while we lie in bed half-naked.

Five minutes later and she would have left. Every touch felt custom made, as if it had been divined long ago for this night. Locking lips and enchanted stares into eyes that could stop any healthy man's heart.

I move closer to her under the sleeping bag, the only bedding she could find in her partially furnished efficiency apartment.

I trace my finger along the milky-white skin on her shoulder. It is soft as silk, like the rest of her body.

She has a figure like a naked woman in a 17th century painting—her breasts slight while her stomach moderately round, not fat but not model thin either. I had always found the women in those paintings unattractive, but in real life they are perfect.

I looked at her dyed-black hair and knew I would do anything for her. Earlier in the night she had rolled over with the sleeping bag, and I lay awake shirtless and shivering rather than disturb her slumber.

A web browser remains open on her computer where we had looked up flights to do the El Camino de Santiago.

[Email to Justin]
10:14 p.m.
hey man, im thinking of doing the way of st. james walk to santiago de compostela with this girl, mari. its in spain. its 800 kilometers in spain. 30 kilometers a day. what do you think? are you cool with that? it takes a month, so i will have to change my flight. wish i could see your face right now. hahahaha.

not joking.

[Justin's replies]
12:20 a.m.
You need to do whatever makes you happy. I will not be angry or judge you. Somehow I am fighting with mine. Lol.

12:30 a.m.
You better go, or you will regret it for the rest of your life. My girl and I are arguing right now, what a disaster. I can't leave until I have closure.

3:06 a.m.
What happened to us?!

[Me]
3:29 a.m.
lol um we may not leave until saturday. she wants to see her family first. i do not know what to do. we can still go to tallinn tomorrow and st. petersburg. we can invite this girl to go with us if you want to keep traveling, or she and i could delay our trip until later.

{14}

[Justin]
6:06 a.m.
Okay, I just sobered up and was reading my emails again. Needless to say, I am a little confused. If I understand you correctly, you're taking a month-long journey starting Saturday? Things are a little weird here at the moment. The situation is . . . fluid. I do not know if I will be back by 2 p.m. or not. Oh, she loved the scarf!

[Me]
11:29 a.m.
I don't think we're going now, and if we did, it wouldn't be until October. Glad she liked the scarf, lol.

[Justin]
11:36 a.m.
Why not? Are you still hanging with her?

11:39 a.m.
I am confused. As of your last email, you were going. What happened?

[Me]
12:00 p.m.
Haha, we were drunk. She got cold feet in the sober morning. Are you coming back later today?

[Justin]
12:07 p.m.
I can't come back today—we had an intense conversation about me taking her to the States and having babies, she said that if asked, she would go. Then we cried together, then we started arguing, and she left. We are meeting today to talk about things. I am not sure how all this happened! Damn Finland!

So, are you going to see yours again? I was thinking of asking Alina to take a trip with me this weekend. If you two are hanging out this weekend, maybe we could all go to Tallinn. Are you still seeing her this week? What do you think?

[Me]
12:53 p.m.
OMG. I think I know how you feel, but maybe we should get out of Finland.

I don't know if Mari would want to go to Tallinn, but she might go to St. Petersburg.

Are you going to be hanging out with Alina the rest of the trip?

Maybe you and I should go to Tallinn for a day or two just to clear our heads. These Finnish women are spellbinding.

I would love to see Mari again, but I'm not sure how she feels. I told her I had someone back home, which cooled her off. And then I might have scared her when I started telling her how much I liked her. Damn wine.

Do I need to come get you? We should probably talk in person before you commit to anything too crazy.

1:01 p.m.
When are you meeting her? I think you should come back tonight, and we should go to Tallinn.

[Justin]
1:34 p.m.
I am meeting her at 4 p.m. I can't come back tonight because I cannot leave with what happened last night. I need some closure. Plus, I need to give her some earrings I bought her. I want to see her this weekend, so that's what I was thinking. You could go to St. Petersburg with yours, and I could go to Tallinn with mine, unless there is a ferry

that runs on Saturday to St. Petersburg. Heck, for all I know, she doesn't want me to stay anymore. I asked her, and she said we would talk about it tonight. So, things are in serious flux here. I will know more after tonight.

1:57 p.m.
There is a Saturday line, but she would have to take a half-day on Monday. I will ask her when I see her.

[Me]
2:20 p.m.
I'm not sure what to do in this situation.

So basically you won't know if or when you're coming back until you talk to her at 4 p.m.?

I kind of feel like I need to come up there. If you do anything extreme, people are gonna be pissed at me for at least not being around. Please don't do anything crazy without talking to me first.

I feel like I shouldn't leave Finland until I know what is happening with you, but I also don't want to overstay my welcome at Reko's.

[Justin]
2:28 p.m.
I'll know more tonight. Most likely I will be on a train tomorrow for Helsinki. I just need some closure. I do not foresee myself staying here since you're not leaving to Spain. I have to do this on my own. I need to do this!

Besides, she might want me to leave after last night.

[Me]
2:30 p.m.
OK. The sooner you can let me know, the better.

[Justin]
2:31 p.m.
Are you not hanging out with your girl anymore?

[Me]
2:32 p.m.
No. I'm back at Reko's. I think she has plans all day.

[Justin]
2:34 p.m.
Are you going to see her again?

[Me]
2:38 p.m.
I don't know. It was hard to read her when I left. Also, she is going north to visit her family at some point.

[Justin]
2:43 p.m.
I meet Alina in 1.5 hours. After we talk, I will know more. I will email you tonight.

3:01 p.m.
Is having sex without a condom when she is not on the pill considered extreme?

[Me]
3:05 p.m.
Yes, but I'm more referring to sending any messages to someone back home about this or committing to something long-term with this girl.

3:08 p.m.
Is she gonna get Plan B?

[Justin]
3:12 p.m.
It didn't happen, was more of a close conversation.

3:13 p.m.
It very well might happen.

[Me]
3:16 p.m.
If you think it might, then you should probably buy some condoms.

What has happened to us? Finnish women . . .

[Justin]
3:29 p.m.
I am on my way to see her. Probably won't be out too late. I will email you when I get back.

{15}

[As the day wore on and my emotions built, I could no longer write, so I recorded my thoughts into a voice memo app on my phone.]

I wish I had taped our conversation. I wish I had recorded her laugh. I wish I'd recorded her voice. I wish I'd recorded the way she says "pasta." I wish I had done all these things.

I'm scared, very scared. I'm pretty sure I fell in love . . . and I'm terrified. I rarely feel any attachment when I have physical encounters with other women. I never expected to have such an emotional encounter. I don't know what happened. I'm scared.

Justin's gone. I don't know how I'm gonna make it through the night. I kind of want to . . . just leave. I kind of want to go back to the States.

I don't know what to do. I didn't mean for this to happen. I didn't know this would happen. I thought it'd be fun to fool around. I didn't, I mean . . . I . . .

Shelly's incredible. I mean, she does everything for me. But I didn't know anything like this girl existed. I don't know that I'll ever . . .

My heart hurts really bad. Usually I hook up with someone, and I'm happy. I left Mari's apartment really sad. Sad for Shelly. Sad because I won't get to see this girl again.

I ruined it by being honest, and now she wants me to go, and she's probably right; I'm sure she's right. I love being with her so much. But can you always just do what is most immediate? I mean, my wife is on vacation with my family right now.

This is a bad, bad, bad night to be alone. I don't know what to do. Maybe I should go into town, to the bars. I'm not sure. This is a really bad night to be alone. I'm feeling emotions I haven't felt in a long time and have maybe never felt.

I don't know what to do. I feel claustrophobic; I feel trapped. I need to leave. I need to go. I fell in love. It was just supposed to be a one-night stand, but now it's much more than that. This is bad.

Perhaps I should go have a drink and try to meet someone else I can talk to and maybe forget about this.

I wish I could talk to Mari, but that would be bad. I didn't mean for this to happen. I mean, I didn't have to approach her at all, but I didn't know it was possible to feel like this. And I don't know that she feels anything.

I thought she was cute, and I wanted to talk to her. I saw her picking up glasses at the bar. Her eyes were so enchanting, so beautiful, that I had to know the name that went with them. I gave her my email, and she actually wrote.

This is gonna be a really, really hard night. I really need to get Justin back, and we need to go very soon. This is not good. This is not good at all. I don't know what to say. I need to leave. I have to go. Oh my god.

"I Didn't Know"

I'm sorry if I hurt you
I never meant to
It was one thing when I cheated with my body
But now I've cheated with my heart

I'm sorry for what I've done
I'm sorry
I'm sorry
I didn't know it would be like this
I didn't know
I didn't know

I just saw a pretty girl I wanted to talk to
I didn't know we'd have so much in common
I didn't know we'd share vagabond souls
I didn't know her eyes would blind me
I didn't know this would happen
I didn't know
I didn't know

"Mari Mi Amore"

I saw a girl with enchanting eyes,
And I had to know her name.
Mari.
Mari.
Her name is Mari.

Ay Mari mi amore
I saw you waiting on tables
I had to speak to you
I had to learn your name

I approached you in a noisy bar
You had a tattoo behind your ear
And I spoke to you
And asked your name
You told me Mari

Ay Mari
I asked for your time
And we met for coffee
And coffee became wine

Ay Mari
We talked for hours
We had so much in common
Vagabond souls

Mari mi amore
I didn't count on this
I didn't know about this

Mari mi amore
I didn't know this could happen

Ay Mari
What can we do?
We met for wine
And I fell for you

What do I say?
Mari mi amore
What do I do?
This feeling so strong
I have to channel it into song,
Channel it into song.

{16}

[Email to Justin]
7:25 p.m.
Any update? I think I really need you to come back, and we need to leave Finland. This girl has got a hold on me in a serious way. I can't think about anything else.

[Justin]
7:57 p.m.
I am coming home tomorrow, first thing in the morning. Bad news though, Alina is coming this weekend to Helsinki to spend the night. Can you email your girl and ask if she wants to hang out on Saturday?

8:02 p.m.
I could try and catch a train tonight if you need me there. I think there is one in an hour.

8:11 p.m.
There is a train that leaves in an hour. Say the word, and I am on it.

[Me]
8:14 p.m.
Thanks man, I really appreciate that. I'm g-chatting with Shelly, so I'm feeling better. Did you already book a hotel room for tonight?

I will maybe email Mari tomorrow or Thursday. I don't want her to feel like I'm hounding her. I think she was going to be visiting her family though.

[Justin]
8:18 p.m.
I did book one, but I am coming home tonight. You can't talk to Shelly all night; you need me there.

[Me]
8:22 p.m.
That's true . . . although I can talk pretty late since they're 7 hours behind.

If you're okay coming back tonight though, it could be good for getting started tomorrow and figuring out what the hell has happened the last few days.

[Justin]
8:23 p.m.
I am okay with it. Also, I need to be back in Helsinki on Saturday, so we need to talk about it, i.e., make a plan.

[Me]
8:26 p.m.
Cool. Let me know when you're on the metro if you're able to use the Wi-Fi on there.

[Justin]
9:31 p.m.
I am on the train to Helsinki. Man, I don't want to leave her!!!!!!!!!!!!!!!!!!!!!!!

[Me]
9:33 p.m.
Yeah, this is crazy. Thanks for the update.

[Justin]
9:34 p.m.
I am seriously considering not going back to the US.

[Me]
9:52 p.m.
We just need to get out of Finland for a couple days and regroup.

[Justin]
11:09 p.m.
Arriving in Helsinki now. Be there in 30 mins. Make sure you let me in.

{17}

[One Day Later]

The situation: Met this girl, she's amazing, and I think I'm in love with her. She is Cohen's "Suzanne." She made me feel things I haven't felt in a long time, or maybe ever.

There are several questions that need to be answered to resolve this situation: What are these feelings? Are these feelings real? Does she feel them too? Are we compatible longer-term and in various circumstances?

What are these feelings? I love everything about her—her laugh, her mannerisms, her eyes, her thoughts, when she randomly speaks Finnish, when she's tired in the morning, when she tells me little fun facts, when she talks philosophy, her art.

Are these feelings real? I'm almost certain they are, but I need to see her again to make sure.

Does Mari have similar feelings about me? This is the big mystery. We could hang out again to see if the connection is still there, or maybe we could have a heart-to-heart conversation. However, if she can't or won't see me, then my only other option is to email her and explain.

Are we compatible longer-term? The St. James walk is the perfect way to find out, kind of like when I traveled with Shelly in New Zealand. For example, how does Mari deal with difficulties such as not having food or finding a place to sleep? There were times when I sensed a potential anger or bitchiness in her. If she is kind of bitchy, I would discover it on the walk.

Questions to ask Mari: What do you want from life? What are your life goals? Are you capable of a long-term relationship, given that you're half-crazy? Or would this just be a fleeting thing? Do you want kids? How many?

If we are compatible longer-term, then some hard decisions have to be made, and Shelly must be told.

I've always wanted someone like Wyatt's girl in the movie *Tombstone*, someone who wants to just go and travel the world.

Shelly is an amazing woman, and we have a great relationship, but there doesn't seem to be much passion. It's all become routine, and I'm hardly sexually attracted to her anymore, although this ebbs and flows. I realize now that I've almost always had one foot out the door in our relationship.

When I was lying next to Mari, I was inspired to write so many things. She's my perfect muse. Mari might be my Yoko, my Courtney Love, my Patti Smith.

If these feelings are real and Mari has them too, then some serious issues must be addressed. What does Mari want, and what does Shelly want? Do Shelly and I take a long break and see if we still want to be together, or do we treat it like a Band-Aid and just end it?

Shelly deserves better than me. I don't know what I provide her. Maybe Mari is right that something is missing in my relationship with Shelly for me to have even approached her.

Maybe Shelly senses this could be happening. Could I actually let her go? Do I let the past and all our shared memories go in exchange for an unknown present and future? For a possible better future? Do I go for extreme passion or a good full life?

Can love and passion make a home, or do you need something more practical, like what Shelly provides? They say, "All you need is love," but is that really true?

Does the fact that I feel I could talk to Shelly about this answer my question? If our relationship is at such a high level, how could I leave her?

Falling in love should be the happiest of experiences, so it is sad that any potential courtship with Mari is plagued by the cloud of pain I may cause Shelly. But for brief moments, the cloud lifts.

Shelly supports me so much and has given me everything she can. However, Mari may inspire more at least in terms of life experience, travel, and writing.

My ultimate goal is to have a full life experience. Is leaving my wife more likely to accomplish this? It's not so much I'm leaving Shelly as I'm going to Mari.

If nothing else, even if Mari didn't talk to me on the Spanish trail, I could still use her as a muse for writing poetry and maybe a book.

I think I know the tattoo I want on my right forearm: Mari in cursive, maybe in Spanish at the end of the trail.

If I'm wrong about my feelings for Mari, then I need to consider making a serious recommitment to Shelly, but will this just keep happening, the desire to be with someone new? Is this experience with Mari an exception, an aberration, or a symptom of a deeper underlying problem in my relationship with Shelly? If Shelly and I had kids, would that heal our bond? Or create/reinforce it? If we moved abroad, would that fix/help it?

For today I'll let these questions ride unless I hear from Mari. Then I'll possibly email her tomorrow to hang out on Saturday. So basically I'll do nothing for the next twenty-four hours except maybe write in my journal.

When/if I tell Mari my feelings, I have nothing to lose since she doesn't know my real name, and either she feels the same or she doesn't. If not, then I go on my way and write about her—songs, poetry, books.

Eighteen hours in Finland: that's all it took for our trip and my whole life to be turned upside down.

I hurt so bad right now. I'm not sure the idea that it's better to have loved and lost applies if you only got to be with the person for eighteen hours.

Have I gone insane? What is wrong with me?

I don't think I ever understood Leonard Cohen or fully appreciated his songs until Mari. She is a Leonard Cohen song. These are the girls he writes about. These are the muses that inspire literature, the goddesses.

She was ready to fall for me, I could tell, but when I told her I was in a relationship, her heart closed to me. I have to write a song or poem about her.

"Compulsion"

Across the room I saw you,
Clearing glasses from tables,
Eyes so enchanting,
so beautiful,
I had to know the name that went with them.

A tattoo behind your ear
intrigued me to come near.
It was too loud to hear
but your voice was soft and cute

and your eyes hypnotic.

I gave you my email
and hoped you'd write . . .

Three days later
we set a time
and met for coffee
which became wine
which became dinner
and then more wine.
Now I wish I could relive that night
a thousand times.

{18}

Mari told me she's a Fennoswede.

I'm alone. Crazy and alone.

"I Care So Much I Don't Care"

I will do anything for you.
Protect you.
Help you.
I'll lie down so you can stand,
But to you I will never lie.
I know you're like a shooting star
across the sky
in a beautiful burst.
And I know you'll probably burn me,
But I don't care.

{19}

<u>Things that have happened so far:</u>

- "How much is 183 cm?"

- "You're never gonna be happy."

- Police with beanbag guns surrounding a disco club.

- A guy sat right next to Justin on the train even though there were two empty rows nearby.

- My freaking out about Justin telling me he went to a strip club with Shelly.

- Expensive drinks in Zurich—$15.50 for a JD whiskey.

- Sprechen Deutsch girl.

- Almost forgetting my Kindle in our room in Zurich.

- Guys lined up in an alley, waiting to be called in, creepy guys with mustaches.

- Justin offered to buy a drink for a girl, and she ordered two—one for her and one for her boyfriend.

- Justin hit on a girl who wore red lipstick, a red shirt, and red fingernails while I talked to her friend who had just gotten the iPhone 4. Her parents work and live in Dubai where she went to an American secondary school.

- Trying to charge Justin's card twice for "Restaurant Bar Pub."

- When we didn't order "champagne" at some sketchy place, they turned up the music to deafening levels until we left.

- About 1.5 hours from the Köln train stop we saw beautiful towns nestled between the river and the hills.

- Emailing Shelly and two others.

<u>Quotes from Justin:</u>

"My life is everything I've dreamed of but nothing I've wanted."

"Sometimes you've got to pin your ears back, light your hair on fire, and just do it."

"We're being chased out of Finland by our emotions. Our emotions are forcing us to leave."

In discussing American defense: "We need to build bombs to blow up their bombs that blow up our bombs to blow up their bombs."

{20}

I can't get Mari out of my head. I'm continuously replaying our time together while imagining all the things I might say to her: *I just want to be in your presence. I want to live in the immediate moment with you. I could listen to you talk forever and look into your eyes for eternity. You exude beauty.*

Maybe at the end of the trip after Justin leaves I'll email her: *Do you want to meet somewhere for a few days? Just hang out, drink wine, and have sex? No strings attached.*

Is there any pain worse than being rejected by a desired lover? Maybe she would have seen me if I hadn't spilled my guts. Now I probably freaked her out.

Maybe I can't separate the emotional from the physical like I thought I could. But I didn't count on all we'd have in common. Or all her other great features.

I should have fucked her. Now I kind of want to hate fuck her.

My heart has been hurt enough that it callouses over quickly once it's cut.

Is my desire for Mari representative of a larger issue? Do I want to start over? Would Shelly be better off without me?

I wish I had taken more time with Mari, not gone all ADD on her—emailing Justin and looking up music videos online—and just enjoyed being with a beautiful woman.

Wi-Fi is killing us all. Justin constantly checks his email and the news instead of embracing his surroundings. Hostels are filled with people online rather than interacting.

When he can't sleep, which is basically every night, Justin listens to the same episode of *Meet the Press* over and over.

{21}

I'm trying to write every morning now.

We wake up when we want. We have no agenda, no time schedule.

Late on a Thursday night, we found ourselves at some bar in Estonia where everyone was ordering plates full of shots, all different kinds of shots. Shots on fire. Shots covered in whipped cream. Drunk people were falling everywhere, and Justin leaned in to tell me that we hadn't got off the plane yet, that I was just sleeping on the plane, and our trip hadn't even started.

"Resa"

I'm old and scared, a life unsung.
I don't want to go home.
The sonnet was invented for girls like her.
I want to stay in Europe.
Home is so boring,
Everything is always the same.
I want to stay in that Helsinki efficiency apartment forever.
Paradise is in a small Helsinki apartment.

Lump in throat
Heart pounding
Strange pain
Feeling sick

Resa Resa Resa
Travel Travel Travel

Paradise is a small messy apartment in Helsinki.
I think I found my soul mate.

I'm so bipolar:
wake up depressed,
have a shower,
then I'm fist pumping the air.
Everything is a roller coaster
UP down
UP down
no in between.

I feel out of control,
but I can't think of a good reason
to be in control.
I have no religion,
no rules.

The words of a New Zealand winemaker whisper off
   Spanish valleys:
"There are no rules."
"There are no rules."

{22}

Everyone was looking at me as if I had already developed herpes on my face.

{23}

Mari told me she wanted a tattoo that read, "Life is a beautiful fairytale." Of course that doesn't necessarily mean it's a perfect fairytale, but it's a fairytale nonetheless.

Justin and I wanted food, but all we found was almonds and hot wine. We're like dogs without leashes at the park. We rarely know the time of day.

I can't point at a map of Europe without thinking of Hitler.

Do I want too much or just what's right? Is this the last time I'll fall for someone else? Do I follow love and passion or practicality? For some reason, the only thing I want in life is to travel the world with that girl and then have Finnish kids. Do I need to see a marriage counselor? Will this just keep happening?

If I did the St. James walk, I could write a book of poetry or record every random thing I've never seen before. I will wait one week and then write Mari on September 29th to make the offer to be her shepherd.

"800 Kilometers for a Painting"

I will watch out for you.
I will give to you
and ask for nothing in return.
If you want to be alone, I will go away.
If you are hungry, I will give you my last apple.

In that time
we can discover
whatever we may
on that journey,
whatever inspiration.
I can write a book of poetry.
And maybe another story as well,
maybe about the journey itself,

or about how life is a beautiful fairytale.

Life is a beautiful fairytale.

If doing this inspires
one painting, one poem, one piece of art
that inspires someone at some point,
then it will all be worth it.

Is there anything more beautiful
than a woman wearing a long T-shirt
and nothing else,
walking around a small apartment?

Her legs were without blemish,
she wasn't totally thin,
but she had no fat.
She was perfectly proportioned,
all woman,
a design of Dionysus,
like a fine wine
perfected through the ages.

All the wars of Europe,
throughout the centuries,
were fought for girls like her.

She searched all over her apartment for a condom:
a bag in the closet,
then the bathroom,
a purse,
another purse,
and then the bag in the closet again.

I imagine us starting on the trail,
I,
madly in love with her,
She,
indifferent towards me.

I don't have rules
I rarely feel bad,
but I'm not a psychopath.
My heart, my mind, my spirit
are hardened,
but they are not granite.

I do feel love
I do go out of my way for people,
Yet, I'm calloused.

I do everything to the extreme.

Gravity is taking effect all over my body,
Yet I am grateful for every moment that I breathe,
Every breath.

Is there any greater pain than unreciprocated love?
Are fairytales by definition supposed to be perfect?

{24}

Will all this be viewed as the ramblings of a madman?

Estonial herpes.

Rising sun, setting moon.

The power of perception: women want what they think you might be.

I'm a moth incapable of resisting the flame; I'm playing with fire. "You got what you needed; now you can go back to your girl."

Being with Mari makes me feel so fulfilled and happy, and yet it makes me feel so sad. Sad because I can't have her. Sad for what I might be doing to Shelly, especially if I could have her.

If I view all of this as inspiration for writing a book or making art, then it's different. Then it's okay; then it doesn't hurt as bad. Then maybe I can suppress, forget.

Idea for a poem: "The Butterfly"

Idea for a book: *Life Is a Beautiful Fairytale: A Positive Affirmation of Life*

When I was around five years old, my dad gave me a cassette tape of the Doors. Whether that shaped me or awakened something that was already there is hard to say.

When I was around twenty-three, I discovered Leonard Cohen. And the artist was permanently awakened inside me. My feelings, my emotions are so strong that I have to release them through art. Maybe everyone has that desire to an extent, the yearning for some remnant of their existence. For some people it must be stronger than others, or perhaps they are simply less fearful of judgment and failure.

{25}

Shelly was my lover. Then I traded a lover for a wife. I did this to her. I forced her and molded her into an assistant. Is that what a wife should be? An assistant? What have I done? She does everything I want and everything she thinks I want.

I traded a lover for a wife, which I then traded for a maid. What the fuck?

Every girl is looking for a prince. Shelly thinks I'm her prince, but am I? Have I become complacent in life? We had it all. We have it all. What am I doing? I've set up this perfect little life. But do you settle on love, compromise on love?

How could Shelly love me so much that she would put up with me and all my shit?

My whole life, I've wanted one ally, one friend, one person I could tell everything to, and I have it—I actually have it—and now I would risk losing it?

I can't just keep jumping from branch to branch.

{26}

I joked to Justin that "I better shave my mustache before we go to the black market, or they might try to sell me a little boy."

Justin and I have made a "three bar rule" so that whenever we're in a new city or one of us doesn't feel like going out, but the other one does, then we have to get a drink at three different bars before we can go home. Almost invariably we'll meet someone by the end of the third drink, and before you know it, we're doing a coat check at some random after-hours club.

Tonight we met an Estonian girl who said the word "fuck" all the time. She was so happy and excited whenever I liked anything that she liked. "Oh, that's so fucking cool!" she'd say enthusiastically.

She wanted to know about up-and-coming bands in America—I was like, *uh, check the Internet.*

{27}

Why would I do the St. James walk? Because I can; I mean, I'm alive and physically able. Why not? To do something epic, something great, something unforgettable.

When should I email Mari? Whatever, she'll probably say no. But whatever, she might say yes.

The affirmation of life will be written by a manic-depressive.

McDonald's is fucking gross. I need to only eat salads. I feel more sick after eating McDonald's two times than after drinking a bunch of alcohol.

Out of money. I hate myself. Tomorrow is going to suck. Tonight sucks. I'm a loser. Loser. Loser. Always have been. I'm in Tallinn. Alone. Bored. I don't belong. Anywhere.

"Again"

Depression.
Sets in.
Again.
Like a rolling thundercloud on a country road:
one night of loneliness,
one night of apathy,
one night of rejection,
and I'm depressed.

{28}

"Everyone Is Fuckin' Doped"

Drug companies,
have their clutches,
in everything.
Everyone
is fuckin' doped.
This is a positive affirmation of life
for manic-depressives and less.
Drug free,
will it work for me?
Probably not,
but maybe someone else,
I guess.

{29}

Everyone is getting drunk. No one reads. Fuck the Brits.

Ideas:
- Song about not being able to leave Helsinki.
- Song about a Helsinki apartment.
- Song about being in love with a girl from Helsinki.
- Song about being in love with two girls.

I would die for her, but you're my soul mate. I love you deeply, utterly, and completely. Even though I can't have you, that does not stop me from loving you. If you said the word, I would follow you.

I think Shelly knows that if she fences me, I will escape, but if she lets me roam free, I will probably come back. I don't know why she loves me so much, but she does.

We have all these possessions we've bought together. When I think of leaving her, for some reason I think of our couches the most. I think of the family Christmas stockings, of our "yard with tree." Photographs. Some forced.

I love Mari for who she is, not for what I can make her. At dinner, I had to look past her to the left because if I looked into her eyes for more than a glance I would be hypnotized.

Does Shelly feel about me how I feel about Mari?

I'm addicted to life experiences. If I keep traveling, will this become the norm? Another city, another love lost.

{30}

I want to go and fill notebooks.

On a Friday night on a Tallinn street, a fire twirler becomes a god.

We didn't go to bed until 4 a.m. even though we got back to our hostel at midnight.

My sexual demons rear their head.

Another morning when I just want to sleep. I want to shoot snorers like wounded horses.

In Tallinn, the party lasts until at least 8 a.m. We can still hear the bass pounding from a nearby club.

We are wasting away in alcoholic dreams of mutual madness.

Quotes from Estonia:

"Out of my way cat; I know who you are."

"If I'm sober, I might not do it, so I'll need to stay drunk the whole time."

"It's a long walk to the town hall; you may get hungry."

"Estonia has badass Terminator-looking cops who are nice when you ask for directions. They probably had sensitivity training 'cause they weren't born nice."

"We serve you well."

{31}

"Wi-Fi Is Killing Us"

Beautiful ocean
and city skyline views
forsaken for a web browser.

An obsessively compulsive
and troubled soul
wasting away on Wi-Fi
and morning beer.

{32}

I've been on the road so long that I've forgotten who I was.

"Longing"

An ocean breeze of love
sails through me like a song
When I wake I think of you
and hope it won't be long

{33}

I'm not afraid to write anymore. I'm not afraid to tell people I write. I'm not afraid to fail.

All the pain that I have squandered in this indelible dream.

"The Butterfly"

The butterfly is free;
You cannot hold her,
only enjoy her
in the moment of bliss
in which your paths cross.

Don't view her going as a loss;
You saw her,
You knew her.
She is the butterfly,
Beautiful butterfly.
Life is short,
But oh so beautiful.

{34}

Hunger and being on the road go hand in hand. You can't always find food, or you don't know how to get it. And you get so tired, you'll fall asleep anywhere—parks, museums, on a rock, anywhere. You just lie down or lean against a wall, close your eyes for a few moments, and soon you're out.

Often, the only times my soul finds peace is when I'm on the move, being transported on a boat, train, or plane. Packing my bag, throwing it on my shoulders, and leaving a town is one of the greatest feelings. I imagine it's similar to what people search for in meditation.

"The Butterfly: Part 2"

You cannot have her.
Only enjoy her.
She is free.
She will make your heart flutter
but you cannot have her.

If you're lucky,
She'll let you in
but don't think you'll stay,
That's not the butterfly's way.

{35}

If I went on the St. James walk, I would try to write metaphoric and anthropomorphic poems about butterflies, birds, and Mari.

"The Bird"

She walks along the ground,
light and free,
always ready,
to fly away from me.

{36}

"Time"

I have a problem:

My parents are aging,

My family is dying,
Yet I'm not around.
I go home, and things are always the same,
but someday, they won't be . . .

{37}

"Ruiner"

For a moment,
all was perfect,
and we were in love.
Then I ruined it.

I had it all,
then I ruined it.

A golden future together,
meet your family.
Laughter,
Wine, chocolate, and laughter.
Then I ruined it.

{38}

Mari said she liked to draw things that are real.

The hunger in my stomach merges with the pain in my heart, and my whole torso hurts.

Babies are not objectively cute.

I look around, and I am the only one writing.

I approached her in a noisy piano bar: "Hey, what's your name?"

"Maha..."

"I'm sorry," I said, leaning my ear closer.

"Mari."

"What's your tattoo?"

"A buddi I."

"What?"

"A butterfly."

"How long will you be in Helsinki for?"

"I live in Helsinki."

"Could I give you my email?"

"Email?"

"I'm traveling, so my phone doesn't work here."

{39}

After Tallinn we returned to Helsinki, and Justin went to meet his girl. Within thirty minutes of being on my own, I got swindled by a guy on the street who asked for money to buy a beer to treat a hangover. It was my fault—I was just standing outside the main train station searching for Wi-Fi on my phone.

The guy smooth talked me into giving him two euros. Once I realized I had been hustled, I wanted to stomp his skull. I wanted to represent the US well, but instead I looked stupid, like a sucker.

Later I saw the guy at the bibliotek and realized I needed to just let it go. I need to get better at letting things go.

When you're by yourself, you've got to get somewhere to regroup, so you're less likely to be a target. I haven't traveled by myself much, so I'm still learning.

There's a lot more time to observe when you're by yourself and thus to write. You can watch people more closely because there isn't the distraction of talking. You notice ugly guys with drop-dead gorgeous girls, single girls strutting and swaying down the street.

You can sit forever in a European café—something I would never do at home.

It's hard to return to a city where you've had your heart broken, to see familiar sites you associate with that person.

{40}

"Would you be okay if she did it?" is always the question girls ask me about Shelly.

"Did you ever believe in God?"

I haven't eaten all day, and it's 3:30 p.m. But I had McDonald's twice yesterday—gross.

Sure I miss home. I love our little neighborhood, playing music with my neighbor. I mean, we just formed the Manner Born. But I have the chance to do something epic and to write from it.

If I went to Spain, I'd also miss out on our trip to Alabama. To dress the part of a NASCAR fan at Talladega would be pretty memorable. But I'm writing so much right now.

Reasons for and against doing the walk:

Pros
1. It would be epic
2. Can write since I'd have a perfect muse
3. Life experience
4. Physical challenge
5. Using my body while it's still relatively young
6. Once-in-a-lifetime opportunity in a lot of ways
7. Giving something to Mari

Cons
1. Can't visit my friend in Bamberg
2. Can't visit my friend in Leipzig
3. Can't go to 'Bama
4. Less time in the neighborhood
5. Can't work on music with my neighbor
6. Book gets delayed
7. Harder on Shelly

***

8:30 p.m. and I still haven't eaten. It's been about twenty hours since I had food.

I'm staying in room 410 of some sketchy hotel.

When you're abroad, most of the time everything is the fucking same, except slightly different. Instead of American football, there's soccer; newspapers look the same, just in a different language; the bars are the same but with different beer. The music, the music is often exactly the same, usually Bon Jovi or something like that.

I don't care about anything you've ever done, the mistakes you've made—I love you. For the first time in my life, I feel like I have a soul mate.

"Helsinki"

I walked the streets in Helsinki
I got lost in Helsinki
I had a shot with long drink in Helsinki
The old are still young in Helsinki

Skip Copenhagen except Christiania
Stockholm is lame
But oh in Helsinki
There's somethin' goin' on

I fell in love in Helsinki
I got my heart broke in Helsinki
I got lost in Helsinki
The people are real in Helsinki
They know how to drink in Helsinki
Everyone has tattoos in Helsinki

I fell in love in Helsinki
I got my heart broke in Helsinki
I walked the streets in Helsinki
I crouched down and wrote this song in Helsinki

The people are mad in Helsinki
The people are a drunk mess in Helsinki
Goddamn I love Helsinki

The most beautiful women are in Helsinki
Take a trip to Tallinn
But come back to Helsinki

Helfuckinsinki
Helfuckinsinki

{41}

The people move past me on a conveyor belt of space and time.

You can make up a price; I don't care—rip me off.

We are the mad ones; we are the writers.

We don't choose art; it chooses us.

The pretty girls don't want me anymore, my old and wrinkled face.

I have loved four women in my life.

The butterfly angel.

There are so many things I wish I could say to Mari: *I unapologetically love you. If you said the word, I would follow you. I would leave my entire life behind and start with these possessions on my back. You are so beautiful; you make me want to cry. I feel like I have to show you New York. You have so much beauty in you. I feel like it's important for you to see New York soon. I feel like I need to show you things to expand your world. Paris, London, Lisbon, Prague. I think that's my predestined purpose in knowing you, even though I don't believe in predestiny. I've never really wanted to see India before, but I want to see it with you. I want to give to you and ask for nothing in return. I didn't mean to fall in love with you; it was an accident.*

{42}

Another night alone with Kleenex. Fuck me.

I'm trying to regain lost youth. Gravity is starting to take its toll on my face and my body. My days are numbered. I used to party and run.

Last night I went out drinking by myself and went to five bars—no, six bars. At some point I went to a southern-fried chicken place and ordered a burger.

Eventually I ended up at a Finnish punk club that was covered in broken glass. There were all these kids, a long-haired guy sitting Indian style and bobbing his head, a short-haired girl dancing on a table. Many of them will be real estate agents or middle management someday, but for now, they have the one thing money can't buy—youth.

{43}

I hate all my friends' wives.

I hate this girl Justin's with. She's so fucking cold to me. I don't know what he told her, but she's a stupid, dumb cunt.

When we were in Estonia, we met these girls who treated us as if we were trophies to be shown off. It didn't necessarily feel bad, but I didn't like it either.

The butterfly floats along the trail. You have the honor to enjoy her beauty for the moment.

"What Could Be"

We could be
So much more
If you would let me
Through your door

{44}

Helsinki sunlight.

"..."

I'm sorry
for what I've done to you.
I wish
I didn't have to.
I never knew
this could happen.
An accident
of the heart.
I wish
there was a way ...

{45}

"Dial Tone"

Cold and alone;
I sit by the phone;
Waiting for a call,
that will never come.

{46}

Maybe you don't marry girls like that.

What would Mari do, if she only knew?

You don't have to worry; I'm crazy but not insane.

A cigarette with coffee is a joy I have never known.

At a Helsinki park, everything is the same, right down to the loitering Negroes marking me from a distance.

The sun shines through a fountain as beautiful red flowers savor the last days of fall, and school children play soccer while their parents cheer from the sidelines. Some of these kids will be at the punk club in a few years, their hopes of football glory dashed early on.

"Purity"

Sounds of children playing
fill the air,
Full hearts
without a care.

Minds that have only known sobriety,
something long gone inside a me.

{47}

I wander the streets for hours. A short conversation, lives of random interaction.

At a concert in a crowded Finnish alley, I was compelled to find a corner, crouch down, and write a song. I think I have turned a corner, becoming all that I hoped.

The writing is random, the thoughts from nowhere. I'm merely a conduit to put them on paper. They write themselves if I only listen and allow for an environment of reflection and experience.

No one else seems to be writing. I've never seen anyone write so regularly in public except maybe one friend from home.

"Life Is a Beautiful Fairytale"

Can you see a butterfly?
If not, can you smell a rose
If not, can you feel a human hand
If not, can you solve an equation
If not, when you sleep do you dream,
Can you taste a new flavor
Tap your foot to music
Close your eyes from exhaustion
Laugh? Can you laugh?

Any of these by themselves make life worthwhile;

All of them together, make life a beautiful fairytale.

{48}

The ramparts of our hearts.

Mari is the type of girl who inspires Cohen's songs, and that's why I need her as a muse. I wrote her for the third time today, but she says she is too busy to see me.

I love you without apology.

I cross multiple worlds: the gypsy and the corporate, the athletes and the nerds.

Save me your judgment and malignant stares.

Deep in America.

Everywhere I go in the world, people are on Facebook, and it depresses the hell out of me.

Do I have a right to ask for more when I already have so much?

I fear that someday I will just be an old man filled with regret.

Band recommendations:
- Incredible Nothing from Finland
- Turbonegro from Norway
- The Hellacopters from Sweden
- Paleface, a Finnish rapper

{49}

Justin and I partied until four thirty in the morning on a Sunday night in Helsinki. Being a Sunday, we didn't think we'd be out late, but at the third bar we met some guys who were in a band called Incredible Nothing. One of the guys had a deep baritone voice. He looked like Salvador Dalí and dressed like Picasso. He was with another guy who was truly mad.

After a few games of foosball, they invited us to check out another bar. On the way, the madcap started stomping things on the sidewalk and telling us to join him. When I asked, "What the fuck are you talking about?" the guy dressed like Picasso told me to just pretend I understand.

The guy stomping things seemed like Syd Barrett incarnate. I don't want to be that mad; that crosses a line of sanity. But I did identify with him. I felt a strange kinship standing next to him.

He told us he drove a taxi on a Finnish reality show and he wanted his catchphrase to be, "I'm going to go home and grab a beer."

At a rock 'n' roll bar we toasted "to making friends from other cultures" before taking a shot of absinthe.

{50}

The butterfly, she knows it.

The incandescent rags of funeral parlor games.

She changed the way I listen to music.

At times I am reminded of all the friends I have betrayed.

At Starbucks, you can get an Americano for like $2.20, and it's fucking good. The lady behind the counter won't look at me with her palpable disdain.

"Where are you going to?"

Everyone always asks us, "Why did you come to Finland?" The dudes from Incredible Nothing couldn't grasp it until we told them we were backpackers. That's the only explanation that seemed to somewhat satisfy them.

{51}

Allan Sparks is my Tyler Durden. Would Allan Sparks ever publish anything? It seems not. Matt Coulee would though; he would publish poetry. Maybe Allan Sparks would be in a rock band or something. Or perhaps he's just a one-time pseudonym.

{52}

I think my writer friend from home told me that stuff about his past so that I might truly understand him because it has so shaped him. To open the door, pull away the curtain, and see if I stayed.

Our lives are characterized by excessive drinking.

One of the surprises of this trip is the dancing. So far I've danced two nights in Helsinki and one in Estonia.

I had an overwhelming feeling as I was booking the hostel for St. Petersburg; it suddenly dawned on me that I was going to Russia. Russia! That's some next-level shit.

***

We're on the boat to St. Petersburg. There is an amazingly cheap-looking show on the TV about ship safety. The main character is named Mr. Safe. The song "Can't Help Falling In Love" is playing throughout the ship. Interesting. She changed music for me.

Justin and I have made plans to stick together, to act like we know where we're going at all times, to not speak too loudly, to disguise our nationality, and very importantly, to not drink too much.

I can't understand any of the words that are spoken around me.

{53}

The diamonds of the night and a whistling prayer.

Art reflects the human experience, and artists, in order to improve and often sell their craft, must have new experiences or go and engage experiences and feelings that are unpleasant or which take them to where other people are afraid to go, so they can be reflected and appreciated in the medium. Art must create an emotion or a thought in the audience. To laugh, think, cry, dream.

"Writing"

Writing, Writing,
Always Writing,
Striving,
For a Dionysian dream.

{54}

The thread that holds my sanity seems to be getting thinner. Or perhaps I'm just more aware of how thin it's always been. I hope it will never snap.

"For the Initiated"

Esoteric jokes.
Random thoughts and broken lines.
Tomorrow I will be in Russia.

{55}

In Helsinki, I got heavily hit on by a gay guy on the dance floor.

These scribbled words. If you tell me I'm brilliant, does that make it so?

"The Dwelling Place"

The graces,
of our ages,
Reading,
from Tabernacle sages.

{56}

"The Social Dance"

The butterfly, she knows it.

Minuets of disease
looking for sleaze
. . . and grit.

{57}

Justin told me he used to write but that he stopped when he started taking his anxiety "medication."

"Curse the Pill"

Curse the pill
that changes moods.
Curse the pill
that makes me like you,
that makes you like me.
Curse the pill
that numbs art,
limits emotions,
the highs and lows of life.
Curse the pill
that makes drug companies rich
and turns kids into zombies,
medicating normative deviance
on a whim of ill-conceived ignorance.
Curse the pill.

{58}

"Goodbye"

Trembling hands from a torn heart.
A Helsinki fireside chat.
Kardashian flames of fallen grace.
Distant cities of blackened diameter.
A 360 degree turn in a 16,000 ton ship.

A lighted path
and a blissful dream
A cold Chardonnay
and a silent scream

I see myself,
Sitting Indian style in her apartment;
Writing,
while she paints.

I feel sorry for all landlocked cities,
Say goodbye to Helsinki.

{59}

"Extra Ordinaria"

The halls of darkness,
The shallow halls of darkness,
Drowning in a web of masturbated colloquialisms.

I photographed it with my mind,
We're going to Russia.

{60}

"Łódź Litzmannstadt"

The Russians are coming!
The Russians are coming!
They yelled.
Aye, but so are the Germans.

{61}

Everyone is talking about Berlin.

I'm so tired. I need to turn off my inner voice for a bit. I feel compelled to write nearly everything it says, and I can't walk anywhere because I'm constantly having to take out my notebook.

We're barhopping in the Baltic Sea, the "three bar rule" still in effect.

You don't drink for the beer; you drink for the company, the experience, the hopeful memories. That's what you're paying for.

There's security somewhere. Serious security. Maybe deep in the bow.

Raise your glass to the Russian soul. Their leaders made robots out of people. Decades and centuries of oppression, exterminating anyone with personality outside the norm.

The Hermitage of our lives: when I was 31 years old, I had a torrid love affair with a 23-year-old Fennoswede. What if I don't go back to the States so I can write a poem about an anthropomorphic butterfly?

"Female Assassin"

Choke me with your words
Drown me with your thoughts
Shoot me with your eyes
Stab me with your thighs
Starve me with your mind

{62}

Justin and I frequently have long conversations about what makes Americans distinct. America—what a beautiful word, les États-Unis.

Miami and DC, all those cities. When I'm abroad, even Mexicans remind me of home.

The Nutty Professor is playing on TV, translated into Russian. How the fuck can the Russian language capture Negro barbershop humor?

You can say I'm racist, but I'm not.

Tomorrow we arrive in St. Petersburg.

To do the St. James walk or not? Artistically I don't think I can say no. It's such a good opportunity, one that I don't think I'll ever have again—to have a beautiful woman that I love to write about. I'm writing like mad, and Mari changes the way I hear music. She inspires Leonard Cohen songs, and I need that type of muse.

I need to talk to Shelly about it. I would like to go on a cruise with Shelly. If I left Shelly, I would miss all our pet names and inside jokes—Mr. P. and brow nuzzling, the protruding brow and myriad others. Also, there are a lot of friends I won't get to see if I go on the walk.

But then I think about art and writing—I just don't want to regret not going the rest of my life, missing the chance. I could get inside Mari's mind and learn what she thinks about everything. And two nonreligious people doing an 800-kilometer religious walk is ridiculous.

<u>Quotes from my family and me:</u>

"Hey there, have you seen Sprinkle? If you do, tell her we're looking for her."
—My dad to the neighbor's dog while searching for our dog.

"Look, Emily, a giraffe."
—My dad to my three-year-old niece while pointing at the family dog.

"Don't bring them around till they're house broken."
—My grandmother to my mom regarding me and my siblings.

"I want to give her my dick."
—My current thoughts regarding Shelly.

{63}

Mama, your boy from Iowa is in Russia.

"Nineteen years in Paris and I wasted my life."
 —A guy who never left the couch at our hostel.

"Wonder"

Standing,
At the Hermitage,
In the rain.
My life,
Will never be the same.

{64}

<u>The Hermitage</u>

- Overpowering, stunning, awe-inspiring, a pain in the ass to get into.

- Never seen anything like it. Makes me want to see the Taj Mahal and other famous wonders.

- Makes me want to cry, heartbeat increases, still stunned.

- I feel so small.

- I feel like I need to rethink my entire worldview.

- Naked children holding hands.

- How could anyone live their whole life without seeing this?

- The fatigue of the road vanishes in moments like these.

- I feel like I begin to understand why Russia became so state-centric when I think about how many times they've been invaded.

- At an allegory of poetry, the tour guide on my headset stated, "Music is inseparable from poetry" and that "a poet ought to be in love."

- In all these things I am fulfilled.

{65}

A mother's hope for her child, there are few things more beautiful than an infant suckling on a mother's breast.

Heavy eyes on a tired chair, how long must you stay there?

Barbed-wire lies, for your words you now must die.

My greed couldn't leave me satisfied with just one night. *Tell me everything about you; don't leave out a single fact.*

"The Field"

Beyond the limits
of human thought.
In the realm
of what is not.
I go to find
the furthest reaches
of my mind.

{66}

A shivering walk.

"Yearning"

The moth and the flame:
I am the moth
and she is my flame.
For her I so yearn,
I don't care if I burn.

{67}

"Waiting"

Remnants
of communist dysfunctionalism,
inefficient recidivism

As I stand here and wait,
Troops
march through the Brandenburg Gate

Conquer Conquer
Berlin,
The new city of sin.
March—
To the Moscow winter.

{68}

Short stories on hostel etiquette in St. Petersburg

"It looks gay, but it's functional."
—A Venezuelan with a roller suitcase/backpack who couldn't leave Russia because of a visa issue.

A flamboyant man complains he wasted nineteen years of his life in Paris. He hasn't left the couch all day. When the television shows the temperature for various cities, he loudly makes obvious statements about the weather for that particular place. "Oh, 20 degrees in Rio, that's cold," he says with such a lisp the couch could catch on fire. "When it's 20 in Rio, the people wear fur coats, but when it's 20 in London, they go to the beach."

Another guy is super nice to us in the morning and then acts like he doesn't know us in the evening. But who is he? Just some pseudo-artist wigger from England. "I take photographs." *Sure you do.*

An Italian, who else, strategically places cologne and painstakingly chooses just the right shirt for baiting Russian women.

Justin passed out early with help from vodka and Valium. I stayed up to do our laundry. When I finally got to bed, I tossed and turned for about two hours over the sounds from the hostel bar where the Venezuelan was boisterously retelling his visa story. "They won't let me leave 'cause I don't have a visa! But Venezuelans don't need a visa to visit Russia! If I need a visa and don't have one, then how did I get in?!"

I finally fell asleep around 4 a.m. only to have Justin wake me at 6 a.m. to ask if I'd taken the laundry out of the washer. I had never been so mad at him. I punched the pillow several times and stewed angrily for fifteen minutes when suddenly the door flew open and the lights burst on. Rico Suave, the Italian, had to pack for his flight.

It looked like he was wrestling a bear as he tried to close his absurdly large suitcase, beating his clothes inside while thrusting his entire body weight against the top. Through half-open eyes, I asked if his night had been successful, and he told me it was.

After the Italian left, Justin came over to my bunk laughing and said that I could no longer be mad at him for waking me up. I laughed too, knowing he was right.

{69}

The album *High Violet* is my sanctuary, has been since April.

I want to take back the four years I lived in Miami and hit reset to a 1984 birth under a different name. I didn't enjoy or experience life during those four years; all I did was work. My heart, my life, is on the road.

I owe Justin 250 rubles and 7 euros.

A life so sad, so hard, so Russian. In visiting St. Petersburg decades of perception and stereotypes are both confirmed and proven wrong.

I imagine great Russian factories defeating Nazis.

In the stairwell of St. Isaac's Cathedral, people had thrown coins on a windowsill as if they could buy their prayers.

At a café where no one spoke English, we pointed at an order for something called "herring under the fur coat." It was good.

If we made this trip into a movie, it would start when I'm emailing Justin to come home from Kouvola, begging him: "I need you to come home tonight."

A hostess on the boat was rather flirtatious with both of us, and as we walked away Justin said, "She's probably thinking, 'Thank God I have two holes.'"

"I don't wanna lie . . . too much."

"Virulence"

Lives characterized by intoxication,
we eye every woman.

Whiskey, Valium,
an early night

Meet for coffee,
or meet for "coffee"

Time and all its limitations
determine so many of my actions.

I want music I can't understand;
Instead, all I get is foreign sitcoms.

{70}

"Dear Snorer"

To the snorer,

Fuck you.
How many nights have you ruined?
How many girlfriends lost?
I don't care if you can't help it.
Fuck you.

{71}

"Monodrama"

I am the boss and the worker
I am the writer and the reader
I am the general and the infantryman
I am the watcher and the watched
The liked and the disliked
The fucker and the fucked

{72}

I wonder how people in Europe perceive me. Some strange guy, writing, scribbling?

I dealt with the same passport lady going into and out of Russia. I told Justin that "I think we probably would have hooked up under different circumstances."

What has happened to us?

Does Shelly know she's losing me?

Even though I'm in Russia, I don't know what I value more, my notebook or my passport.

Drink a glass of wine and just listen.

"Whiskey Dreams"

Nazi occupation
and a whiskey dream,
making things
not as they seem.

Soviet genocide
for the working class,
a culture of ignorance
in a cognac glass.

Whiskey dreams
emotional vaccines
lantern lights
open bar fights.

Russia
Russia
Mother Russia
What have you become?

Did the Americans do this to you?

{73}

Do I view Russians differently now? Probably; they aren't all *Rocky* villains and nightclub bouncers. Scrawny troops, a generation gone.

I want to find a park, so I can take a nap. I fell asleep on the bus to the boat, utterly exhausted from being on the road. If you travel long enough, eventually it will catch up to you, and you'll fall asleep anywhere.

Right now I'm sitting in a chair on the boat with activity all around, passing in and out of sleep.

There is no escape from goddamn cell phones.

***

I sleep and I'm back, refreshed and ready to go. Sometimes a few minutes is all it takes.

I love Coke—not that kind; I mean the Cola, which may be just as addictive.

I really want a goddamn Snickers.

Who is the mysterious writer, and what is he writing? A journalist? A weirdo?

No one seems to pay much attention to people in Europe. No one looks twice at my writing. In the States I feel like they would.

I need to write with a fury and passion heretofore unknown—to liberate myself.

I wonder what will be the last words I ever write. *Shelly, I'm sorry. I love you. You provide my umbrella, my umbrella for writing, umbrella for loving, for life.*

The St. James walk would be an extraordinary opportunity no matter what. Even if Mari doesn't like me and nothing happened between us, at the very least it would be incredible to get to know another person so fully and completely, especially a person from another country.

I have the complete love of an amazing woman—what is wrong with me?

I'm so fucking cold—broken, cold, and damned.

{74}

"Who knows what's gonna happen on this boat?"

"Just go with it."

"Does rape count if it's an Aussie?"

Every few minutes the loudspeaker on the ship announces that a lounge on the top deck "invites you to our hot parties."

"Ladies and gentlemen, place your bets."

We're backpackers, going wherever the road takes us. We arrive and then we leave. I'm just a stranger in a hood. A mad Russian is blasting me with hate. Maybe because I'm just passing through.

The shipyards of Russia seem endless.

I emailed Mari from an Internet café on the boat. She said she would see me again! I'm beside myself with emotion. The feeling is overwhelming. A second chance. Same place. Her eyes. See her standing there. Will I have the same feeling? Spain?

I wish I could give Shelly all the money in the world, but it still wouldn't be enough for what I might do to her. My heart is torn, and I don't know what to do. There are five weeks of recorded *Daily Shows* waiting for me at home.

I want to see every opera, taste every fruit.

"Diplomatic Relations"

The anticipation
Palpitating heart
I made out with a Russian last night.
It meant nothing
It meant everything
I had to make out with a Russian.
We didn't speak the same language,
but we understood each other perfectly on the dance floor.

{75}

Since a previous attempt at explaining my feelings to Mari didn't work, I decided to try to appeal to reason. At a random café near the port, I asked a stranger if I could borrow a piece of paper.

September 29, 2011

Dear Mari,

After giving it a lot of thought, I would like to go on the walk in Spain with you. If I could make my living from anything, it would be from writing. If I were the richest person in the world, I would still write. I think the St. James walk would not only be an amazing physical challenge but would also be a great opportunity to write.

Here are ten reasons why you should consider going with me:

10. I will have no expectations of you.
9. I will watch out for you.
8. It will be difficult to find someone else both willing and physically able to do the walk.
7. I have lots of hiking and backpacking experience in the Grand Canyon and the Rocky Mountains.
6. No one knows what the future holds. For example, what if you had permanently injured your leg when you got hit riding your bicycle?
5. I think we would have good conversations and learn from each other.
4. When you want to be alone, I will go away.
3. I will give you my last apple when you are hungry.
2. It would be a fucking epic adventure.
1. Why not?

Allan

{76}

What a disaster this all is. How often do you get a second chance? I can't say no to Mari. The woman I have at home . . . I don't know what to do.

I can think of nothing else except seeing Mari. I need to love her and for her to not want me. I need to see her and look her in the eyes. I need to look right into her eyes.

She changed the way I hear music. Every song has new meaning. I understand the lyrics so much more. They all make sense as if I've opened my eyes to the world for the first time after only reading about it.

In my pocket I have the letter. I want to remember this moment forever—this walk to see her a second time, not knowing what will happen. This is life.

{77}

I'm drawn to madness. I thought Mari was mad and that excited me.

I told her there was nothing she could say that would offend me. Her response totally caught me off guard. "I'm not even sure that's human."

Is she right? Am I not human? Incapable of being offended, am I not human? That's what she asked me. Am I just a little calloused, or am I Dexter?

As we parted, she said, "I'm glad you were honest with me, Allan." The irony of her words punched me in the gut immediately. I felt bad, but I couldn't tell her the truth about my real name or at least not offer it. If she had asked me, I'd like to think I would have told her.

I thought she was mad, but she isn't.

I thought she was Suzanne, but she's not.

I thought she was twenty-three, but she's only twenty-one. Maybe that's too young.

I thought she was an artist, but it seems she's not as creative as I imagined; she wants to go to school to study nutrition.

"Do you have a hangover cure?" she asked me with puppy-dog eyes.

She said Justin and I seemed like "two sleazy, horny guys traveling around Europe."

Why do people cheat?

"I'm glad you were honest with me, Allan."

I'm in a race against time.

"The Quest"

Searching for meaning and a song,
The road is where my heart belongs.

{78}

I made out with a Russian and accidentally took a condom out of my pocket when I went back to her room.

Is my friend in DC the only one like me, a madcap writer? What did he mean when he said he "used to go visit cities"?

{79}

And so I leave Helsinki for the final time, with closure, good memories . . . and an undelivered letter.

My only regret is the relationship we never consummated.

I'm so tired. It's 7:30 p.m. and I just want to go to bed. Yet here we are at another Finnish port of call, our fourth ferry ride. This time we're on a cargo ship to Gdynia, Poland where we plan to catch a train to Krakow.

A stereotypical old Polish man is standing silent and motionless looking over the sea. The small bill of his dark leather cap protrudes just past his forehead. Oh, what those old eyes have seen.

When you're leaving a city, you're on fire. You have no idea what awaits you in the next town. The ground is moving as you make your way to a bus, ferry, tram, metro, or some other form of public transportation.

We travel with complete abandon, ready to take advantage of whatever the road offers us. At any moment you can meet someone who can change your whole trip, maybe even your whole life.

"Self-Observance"

The streets
The streets

All the strange faces
on the streets—
Moving
Interchanging
Disappearing
Reappearing

Everyone was an extra in our movie,
a *Casablanca* fairytale.

We watched outside ourselves,
Four hugs goodbye,
The epic dreams.
Hearts yearning for life and love.
Life, love, and poetry.

{80}

I have experiences solely to facilitate art.

The butterfly angel, her thighs.

Maybe Americans are the crazy ones, an open-minded nation without rules. Well, at least some of us are that way.

Twenty-one is so young. I probably thought differently then too—wishful thinking and heartfelt desires, perfect relationships and common needs, priceless love and happy lives.

The choice isn't always between happy and unhappy; sometimes it's between happy and happier.

"I'm glad you were honest with me, Allan."

Even though things didn't work out with Mari, it's clear I desire an artist, someone crazy, untamable. A passionate ally, a mad travel partner, fucking in hostels, jumping from country to country.

Did Mari conceal her true self from me? She seemed so mundane, so boring when I met her the second time. I don't think that's who she is. She might actually be an artist. I sensed an artist's soul, not a fucking nutritionist.

Letters of love.

If I type out my journals, then they can be searchable for when I need a line.

Fucking TVs are on constantly.

Heaven is a small apartment in Helsinki.

Even though I lied to Mari about my name and age, I told her the truth about more than I've told almost anyone else. Maybe the two go hand in hand.

"There's nothing you can say that would offend me."

"That's really scary."

"It's true."

"I'm not even sure that's human."

Then later she told me, "Maybe there's something missing if you feel the need to do what you do."

I'm not that sexually attracted to my wife. So what do I do? I don't think anyone would ever love me like Shelly, but she's kind of an Anne when I want an April. Sure there's more to life than sex, but life is short, and I'm sexually bored. I'm tired of sleepy hand jobs imagining someone else.

I'm surprised I was wrong about Mari.

"I Am a Traveler"

Dear God, you know I am a traveler
I travel to the heart
I travel to the soul

Dear God, you know I am a traveler
I travel far and near
I travel without fear

Dear God, you know I am a traveler
Yearning to be free
Yearning to be me

{81}

"Just Go With It"

You cannot know me,
but you can blow me,
for I have a secret life.

I would tell you my name;
but it won't be true.
I would tell you my age;
but it won't be true.

I would tell you my deepest secret thoughts,
and those will,
be real.

Please don't ask me questions
that make me lie.
Let's not talk of home
and the people we know.
Let's just go with it.

I could tell you my name;
but it won't be true.
I could tell you my age;
but it won't be true.

I can tell you my deepest secret thoughts
I can pour my heart out on the rocks
And I won't lie about anything . . . that matters.

{82}

"Wandering"

We raise up the mast of our lives,
Yearning,
for something emotional,
Reaching,
for something unattainable.

{83}

"Live!"

I want to see every opera

Taste every fruit
Visit every city
Walk every street
Fuck every girl

I want to drink life from a fountain,
No! I want to drink life from a waterfall
with open arms and upturned jaw.

{84}

Dear Justin,

If you're reading this, something terrible has happened. Please try to publish my journals as a book of poetry titled *Random Thoughts and Broken Lines*. No worries if it doesn't sell.

This notebook reads continuously from both directions, and the other one is falling apart.

Thanks,

Allan

{85}

On a ferry in the Baltic Sea, I got propositioned for a threesome.

So tired—will I ever get sleep?

"A Vesta of Hope"

An anonymous meeting
Three doubles of Jack
Deep kiss
Ashtray breath,
Things unspeakable for most.
The towel moved!

Forbidden pictures
Private conversations,
What's your name?
If you see me again,
you cannot know me.

Strange goodbyes
Diamond eyes
Velvet thighs
A thin masquerade
of vinaigrette disguise,
Searching for a Vesta of hope
in an ignominious ocean.

{86}

"Give Me Whiskey"

Give me whiskey and I'll curse the TV
Give me whiskey and I'll threaten to invade a country
Give me whiskey and I'll join you in your room
Give me whiskey and I'll kiss an ashtray
Give me whiskey and I might turn gay, for a night anyway
Give me whiskey and I'll do anything

Give me whiskey and I'll dance
Give me whiskey and I'll dance alone
Give me whiskey and I'll dance alone in front of everyone
Give me whiskey and I'll join you both in your room
Give me whiskey and I'll howl at the moon
Give me whiskey and I'll sleep until noon

{87}

I'll tell you everything about me except who I really am.

"Be careful, you don't want any germs," I joked as we shared a Coke the next day.

"Can I kiss it?" I asked. Then I did before she answered, "Yes."

"Ink Kisses"

Gypsy souls
intertwined,
Kiss a tattoo
a second time.

{88}

The road glows with limitless potential. Unseen nationalities. Anything can happen.

Goddamn, Poland is cheap.

<u>Music recommendations:</u>
- Devin Townsend, *Ocean Machine*
- Strapping Young Lad (Townsend's band)
- Testament
- Zakk Wylde
- Faith No More

{89}

"Polish Trains"

Clik a Clak, Clik a Clak, Clik a Clak
A train rushes by into the Polish darkness
Will Polish trains ever be separated from Nazi nightmares,
German soldiers
barking orders
to hungry cargo.

Real or imagined,
You sense the pain,
on a Polish train.

{90}

"The Old Train"

Heaving, Heaving,
the old train
moans along the tracks.
Outdated infrastructure,
Vintage—
Sixty years ago.

{91}

"Altruism"

Stranger, Stranger
Thank you for your help.
Stranger, Stranger
I don't know what I'd do without you.
Stranger, Stranger
How can I repay you?

You be the Stranger someday.

{92}

Unconsummated love, the unfinished business of the heart ... and the loins.

If this trip ended now, it would be unbelievable, but I still have two weeks left.

You don't even know the shit I've done. Another day, another city. Distant lights and small towns.

Berlin is calling my name. There is something going on there. All signs point to Berlin.

"You seem confident. Are you?"

"I think so."

"Have you always been self-assured?"

"No."

"Night Trains"

Writing at night,
by occasional streetlight,
and the moon.
Twisting
Turning
Jerking
Hoping we'll be there soon.
An upright nap,
engines humming me to sleep.

{93}

If I could make $40,000 a year creating art, I would be the happiest person in the world.

"Publish or Perish"

Do I put art ahead of everything?
Ahead of my happiness?
Ahead of the happiness of people I love?
Do I have a choice?
The art is in me, beyond me;
I don't write for me;
I write for something better, greater;
But for me too, I suppose.

{94}

"Annoyance"

Nervous twitches
Obnoxious twitches
Tapping fingers
Clicking pen
lurch lurch lug
and we're moving again

{95}

I am a passenger on the train of life. Somehow I can get away with being twenty-six; could you imagine if it was the other way around, and I looked five years older than I really am?

Songs and poems and books—more projects than time.

We approach an old bridge. Is it safe? Does it matter? As if I could stop the train between here and there.

"Questions to a Traveling Stranger"

Do you love your family?
Do you miss them?
Do you worry they are getting old?
Do you worry they will be too old for you to know them?
That they will go away while you are wandering?
Can we be so calloused to the past, our past?

{96}

Justin asked a stranger, "Do you know where the dining car is?"

"It's either this way or that way," he answered, pointing up and then down the train.

I love reading on an anonymous train, being alone with thoughts and words.

Sometimes on the road I meet other souls like mine.

Ultimately, I think Mari was repulsed by me. She could not accept me for who I am. She couldn't get past her predisposed beliefs. I suspect she even hated me.

I am open to love, and that is most likely a problem. But I am excited to go home.

American culture is a good culture. I'm not saying it's the best, just good, at least compared to the Aussies and Brits.

When my future kids are two and four, I want to live in Spain for a year. When they are four and six, I want to live in New Zealand.

Am I a fraud? Too gypsy for the system, too part of the system to be a gypsy; pretending in all circles, straddling two worlds, belonging in neither, or at least not willing to admit that I do, and take the leap off the merry-go-round.

I need you to read this—it's deep and personal and tragic.

"The Depths"

The scribbled lines
of our times
show the depths of lost souls.

We fuck because we want to.
We sing because we need to.
We write because we have to.

We travel out of necessity,
Complacency is a parasite,
gnawing at our souls,
eating our well-being
and desire for life.

Only through travel,
through escape,
through moving on,
do we find momentary peace.

{97}

"Genealogy"

My father was a gypsy with clipped wings,
running along the ground,
chasing a golden spoon he didn't want,
to impress a mother who would never care.

My mother,
raised a gypsy on a leash,
in a mental cage,
and once free,

no distance was too great,
for the steel bars of judgment
will suck the soul.

{98}

We have only one corporeal life. There is no evidence of an afterlife or reincarnation. I am getting old. I will die. Thus, all I have is my life.

My life exists in my brain and is composed of my knowledge, experiences, and memories. Since experience almost invariably includes new knowledge and memories, I want to experience as much as I can for as long as I can.

Life experience should only be turned down if it would limit other life experiences for an overall net loss in life experience. In other words, there is a balance between experiencing life and staying alive to experience more life. For example, jumping out of a plane without a parachute would be a thrilling experience, but it would eliminate the possibility of all other experiences.

In general, jobs and money should only be used as tools or a means for experiencing life.

Of course happiness is an important consideration in experiencing life. After all, in a way, the most fundamental goal in life ought to be happiness. However, a quest for happiness raises two important issues.

First, there is the red pill, blue pill dilemma. Would you rather know something and be unhappy or not know and be happy? I personally feel obligated to choose knowledge. Indeed, what is the virtue of happiness if it's an illusion?

Second, scientific studies have consistently shown that humans are not good at predicting what will make them happy.

Therefore, life experience is most likely a more honorable and attainable goal.

{99}

On the road, a good night's sleep is worth its weight in gold.

My heart fills like a balloon on a night train, and for the moment I am happy, content in my being, at peace within myself . . . yet still I cannot help but think of the walk we'll never take.

"Ode to *High Violet*"

High Violet is my therapy, my God, and my Savior
When I'm bored—*High Violet*
When I'm tired—*High Violet*
When I'm sad—*High Violet*
When I'm alone—*High Violet*

{100}

I fall asleep, notebook by my side, pen in hand. Berlin is calling my name.

"Poisonous Permeation"

Veiled criticism
Passive aggressive insults
Ignorant stupidity
Dictation
under the guise of conversation,
Manipulation,
massaging the truth
changing the truth
inventing the truth,
pill pill pill
liquor wine beer,
mind in a fog,
perpetual fog.

{101}

If something doesn't fit in your pack, you don't need it. Take only what you can carry. Throw things away; take a digital picture, and throw them away.

If you need to sleep, you can stuff your clothes in a pillowcase and use a towel as a blanket.

The scene outside my train window looks fake, like a Hollywood movie set, a cardboard skyline, extras pretending to be in a hurry on a busy railway platform with intermittent screaming children and low-grade miscreants.

We're passing through the Polish countryside, and the previous night is only mentioned by making opaque references to the Baltic Sea. It was weird, but what's even stranger is that it wasn't more weird.

Graffiti seems to be universal.

Universal graffiti.

Grafitti: the common language.

He told a story like the steel beams of an old railway station.

I'll do anything if I can get a poem out of it. Everything is worth it if it fosters creation.

I don't care about money at all. I only care about the road.

The hunger in my stomach makes it so I can't think.

I might be chasing love and passion and that's bad. I will always regret not sleeping with Mari; I should have been prepared.

Mari's certitude about life did piss me off a little. I thought she was crazy too, but apparently she's not.

Old and dreary along the tracks, daydreaming out my window. I look in her eyes. *You and I have unfinished business.*

What do you mean?

I lean in slightly. *You know exactly what I mean.*

I love you desperately.

"A Patriotic Flash"

I bleed red, white, and blue
My heart thumps "The Star-Spangled Banner"
through and through

{102}

We met one of our first Americans on the trip shortly after we arrived at our hostel in Krakow. It's hard to explain the bond you feel for another American on the road. You have each other's back. It doesn't matter—race, creed, color—you're cut from the same cloth, a pattern other nationalities can't fully comprehend. You will stand back to back in an alley with someone you just met as if you'd known them for decades. There's an indelible bond of recognizing the accent you never knew existed and the thrill of being able to speak and understand someone colloquially.

That evening, the hostel took a group of us on a pub crawl. Justin went home early because he wanted to visit Auschwitz the next morning. I stayed out with our new American friend, Mark, whose ancestry is Korean.

Partway through the night, a racist Irishman started hassling a member of our group who was from Bangladesh. The Irishman would ask him things like, "How'd they ever let you into Europe?"

Mark and I tried to reason with the guy, but he wouldn't listen. So I pulled him aside and politely reminded him of the days of "Irish Need Not Apply." Soon he turned his hatred towards me, repeatedly telling me to "shut up and walk away." It took everything I had to hold my tongue and my fists. Thank god I hadn't had any whiskey that night.

After that, Mark and I abandoned the group for our own adventure. We met two pretty Polish girls and danced with them for the rest of the night and into the early morning, over five straight hours.

The girl I was with had beautiful sandy hair that occasionally flipped up in the cutest possible way when she danced fast. Often she and I were the only two people on the dance floor. We barely touched and that made it all the more sensual.

Our time together had been nearly perfect, and I was completely content. Yet as we prepared to leave, I felt obligated to try and sleep with her.

"I have a boyfriend," she told me.

"That's fine, I respect that," I assured her, trying to be a nice guy. Then about a minute later, I couldn't help but add, "If you want to hook up though, no one has to know."

Right before we left, at around 7 a.m., she looked at me with deep enchanting eyes and said, "You have a mustache."

I think I need to start shaving against the grain.

{103}

On the top bunk of a busy hostel dorm room, I write.

I wonder when and how the hostel movement started.

Soon Justin and I will part ways. My road goes on while his has reached an end, back to a life of work and bills. When you're backpacking with someone, you do everything together—you eat, you sleep, you meet people, you sit together for hours and hours on railway cars, but ultimately, the journey is personal as all life's journeys are.

When I'm alone, I write more. Silence alone is blissful yet also painful.

You can know me on the road. People of the road understand my sexual proclivities. I am mad. Are you?

My dick screams for companionship. *Let's lose our rings and become who we truly want to be. I want you to know yourself.*

It seems like everyone on the road is either atheist or agnostic.

I'm going to Berlin to feel the pulse of the city.

"Ode to the Road"

We met as strangers and parted the same,
I never even knew her name.
When you're on the road long enough,
the days, the cities,
and sometimes even the girls, run together.

You sleep when you're tired
You eat when you're hungry
You don't plan
You just go with it.
Everything is all about the moment.

{104}

Mark's 80/20 description of Aussies: "You're with them 80 percent of the way until the last 20 percent when they say, 'Hey, lets get drunk, throw up, and get in a fight.' And then you're like, 'What?! No!'"

Mark and I clicked right away. It's so weird how that happens. As one person said to us, "You seem like you've known each other a long time."

"We just met today."

"Today?!"

It happens everywhere we go—typically we meet girls when Justin goes to the bathroom or gets a drink, and I approach them alone.

"You have a mustache." Maybe the Polish girl didn't want me. Maybe she didn't like me. Or maybe she really did have a boyfriend.

Life would be much easier if I settled down and had kids. Why am I pushing the envelope? Maybe it's not in me like it is in others. Maybe I'm pretending. Maybe I'm just scared at the moment.

I want to open my heart, my soul, my mind, and embrace the experience of life.

"For Shelly"

I want to party with you in Prague
Get high with you in Amsterdam

Walk with you in Copenhagen
Drink with you in Paris
Eat with you in Venice
Live with you in Berlin
Smoke with you in Seattle
Sleep with you in San Francisco
Lie down with you in Iowa
Play with you in Boston
Hold hands with you in Maui
Drive with you in Hong Kong
Sing with you in Barcelona
And this is just the beginning . . .

{105}

For the moment, I feel satisfied. Is it permanent?

To do:
1. Get pictures from Justin
2. Put my pictures on Justin's computer
3. Do a balance transfer
4. Book Auschwitz tour
5. Figure out how to get to Berlin
6. Prague

Maybe I'm not too old; maybe it's not too weird. I felt accepted here.

"I'm glad you were honest with me, Allan."

I miss Mari's laugh.

An epic journey is coming to an end: the things Justin and I have seen, the things we have done, will bind us forever.

We're all waiting for the doctor to call us with bad news.

Mark recommends reading Viktor Frankl.

And the racist mick need not apply.

Things cause me such pain, such emotion, that I can only deal with them through writing. Without that, I would explode.

This has been the strangest, most amazing experience of my life. Tomorrow I see Auschwitz.

"The Soldier's Hands"

The soldier's hands,
and the life they took,
The trench they dug,
and the bombs they dropped.
The soldiers' hands will never stop.

{106}

Krakow is busy and full of energy. I danced for five hours with a Polish girl until we fell into the light at 7 a.m. I was way more drunk than I wanted to be and spent part of the night trying to sober up. I realize now that I somewhat blacked out, and I regret that.

Mark and I ate a döner kebab before stumbling home to our hostel during the morning rush hour.

The girl did seem hesitant to look me in the eyes most of the night, so it kind of makes sense that she had a boyfriend.

I've never danced so much in my life as I have on this trip.

Tomorrow the road becomes a Y, and Justin will leave. I don't know where my path goes—Prague, Berlin, another night in Krakow. Eventually our roads will remerge in DC.

I did pretty well on my goals for the trip. It has definitely been memorable; I've had lots of new experiences, and we've laughed a ton.

I've also done a decent job of going with the flow . . . most of the time at least. I could have relaxed a bit more.

I was okay at changing unpleasant situations.

I won't miss the snoring. Jesus Christ. I suspect he took a Valium tonight.

I did well at taking mental snapshots, but I wish I had taken more. I will take more.

I did a pretty good job of recording conversations with my phone although oftentimes it stopped recording when the screen went to sleep.

I've gathered lots of material for a novel and may have even written a book of poetry.

We only had one big fight, and that was the first night after a bunch of whiskey and a comment about Shelly. Things got a little nitpicky after Tallinn, but it was probably more fatigue or my irritation at having to go back to Helsinki. I was a jerk sometimes, and he would get argumentative. All things considered though, we got along amazingly well. But I wish it had been a little better.

Now there is only one goal left to meet ...

"Polish Girls"

Pretty girls
Pretty girls
Pretty Polish girls

{107}

Open your heart, your mind, your soul to the experience. Embrace the extremity of your emotions. This is life—the experience of emotions.

There is a video playing on the bus ride to Auschwitz. The mass killing of humans. We do the same thing to cows, sheep, and pigs. What's the difference? I guess we eat them or use them for resources and products. We don't kill them purely for the sake of extermination. We don't kill them out of hate. We do pharmaceutical tests on animals though. Maybe the gratuitous suffering is the difference.

A slaughtered infant flashes across the screen, head and feet burnt like wood on a pyre. "Look at it!" he screamed. "Don't look away! Look at it!"

The bus is full of heavy hearts, unable to smile, all silent.

"Guards treated the prisoners like animals." Are we that different from animals? We cry, I guess.

If one prisoner escaped, ten from the barracks were starved to death. They used their humanity against them.

Is a number really that different from a name? They're both just ways to identify someone.

I don't think I could smile now if I tried.

Why the torture? To keep people in line?

My lips are stuck together. Expressionless. I cannot move them. Weird.

I'm not sure that I am normal.

What is the appropriate length of time for somberness?

The road is lined with tour buses to tragedy.

After seeing Auschwitz, I feel like I never have the right to be depressed again.

Some places every human should see: Amsterdam, the Hermitage, Auschwitz, New York City.

Quotes from the Auschwitz tour:

"Shoes of the departed."

"Indirect extermination."

"Date of arrival, date of death. Date of arrival, date of death. Date of arrival, date of death."

{108}

I was so mentally and emotionally exhausted after Auschwitz that all I could do was sleep on the ride to Birkenau. The tour was heavy, almost overwhelming, but I was never really close to crying. It seemed appropriately depressing. The most shocking thing was the piles of hair and shoes.

Looking at the guard towers, I sensed Auschwitzian nightmares, members of the SS pointing machine guns at frail bodies. And for the few prisoners that escaped, I imagined guards in the deep dark woods hunting humans.

I should probably read *Mein Kampf*.

Would you go to a Hitler rally if you could? Just to see what it was like?

"If These Woods Could Talk"

If these woods could talk,
what would they say?
Cries of pain
Fear
And heavy breathing.
Barking dogs
And frantic eyes.
Shouted words
And soldiers' boots.

Then silence,
palpable silence.

Somewhere,
In the distance,
I hear music.
Like flowers in the sidewalk.

Hopes, dreams, love, life
swirling out of a chimney,
evaporating
into the Polish air.

{109}

I had intended to be on my own by now. But instead Mark and I decided to take a night train to Prague together. I'm not sure what to do. This part of the trip was supposed to be an experiment to see how I would do by myself. I also wanted to meet a girl, get a hotel room, and fuck for a week. Now I might only have two days to meet someone.

If I go to Berlin as a solo traveler at the end of my trip, maybe I could meet a girl who is also traveling alone. Mark is pretty interesting and going to Prague with him gives me the chance to learn more from him and to further discuss Auschwitz.

Listen to the road. What is it telling me? The road tells me I just happen to meet this cool dude right when Justin leaves, and he's going to Prague where I was thinking of going anyway.

I just want to make sure I leave enough time for Berlin because if I meet my friend Tara in Bamberg and then my other friend in Leipzig, I won't have much time left.

I could also test traveling with Mark to see whether he might be a potential travel partner. I don't know. If I'm not chasing girls though or traveling alone, I might as well be traveling with Shelly.

I found out Mark is a writer . . . or aspiring writer. He is also a big proponent of the idea that a person is the average of the five people they hang out with the most. I wonder if that works in reverse, to see who you are; or forward, to see who you want to become.

In general, I am doggedly honest . . . or at least I wouldn't lie about anything that matters. I wish I hadn't told Mark I was in a relationship. Stupid. Lesson learned. I can either let people know who I really am or what I appear to be, professional or private life, but not both.

Someone at the hostel in Krakow stole over a hundred euros out of Mark's pack.

It seems like there are a couple types of people who travel. There are the people who want life experiences, the nomads, and then there are the debauchers and assholes, blue-collar dicks with passports—these are the ones who violate the backpackers' code of not stealing from a fellow traveler.

The Americans I meet on the road are usually great. I've still never met an Aussie I liked. They all seem to fall under the debaucher/asshole category.

I want to travel while I still look young enough to approach any girls and not creep them out so that they'll actually talk to me and maybe hang out with me.

I was tired of the road for a moment, but now I'm feeling recharged. I'll probably go home for about five months and then go back out on the road.

There is a 90 percent completed manuscript waiting for me at home. Also, I love playing basketball with the guys from the neighborhood. However, I need to travel and do all that before it's too late, before time takes its toll.

My parents told Shelly's parents that I would never work a nine-to-five job. How did they know that? I wish I had discovered myself sooner.

{110}

And so I leave another city.

The Polish houses around Krakow are surprisingly big and have nice yards. Several of the yards contain chickens.

I've never understood people who discriminate, especially when they come from an ancestry that has historically faced discrimination itself. Do I love Irish people? No, not really. But I told that guy I did. I love the trip I took to Ireland. Dublin sucks just like Madrid and Zurich.

The Beats and the dreamers.

A lot of this journal is gathering phrases to use in other writing.

Evil man, it's not too late to change your ways. We don't need your gas chambers. I'm not religious, but Jesus was right about at least one thing—Matthew 7:12.

Seeing Auschwitz made me want to support American military strength, so we can mitigate the chances of something like that ever happening again. Like Justin said, "Fuck the Swiss," for being neutral in the face of that. Fucking chameleons. Maybe some things are worth fighting for, dying for. Maybe self-preservation isn't always the most important thing.

Mark says he's been told that when NATO forces have to engage the enemy in Afghanistan, they "call in the Americans."

I need a new pen.

{111}

My life is ridiculous, maybe because I'm living two of them.

"No One Knows"

The Baltic Sea
and whiskey.
Dark nights
and Russian girls.
Vagabond hearts
and gypsy souls.
Where we wander,
no one knows.

Town center
and the square of desire.
Drunk man on the sidewalk
making inebriated sounds,

barely audible words
about how things used to be.

Drunk man on the sidewalk
yelling in slurs,
something about the government
and what they deserve.

{112}

When I get home I need to make sure to type all the voice memos I've recorded on my phone as part of my journal. They also might be helpful for a book or for lines I can draw from.

Talking, talking, so much talking. I've never done so much talking as I have on this trip.

In our sleeper car on a night train to Prague, Mark and I have deep conversations about travel and what it means to be American.

Americans dominate every new industry. It's amazing. Facebook, Google. We dominate the old and the new. How? Ingenuity, hard work, something else?

Things that Mark has recommended:

Sweet camera:
- IXUS 115 HS

Epic places to visit:
- Angkor Wat in Cambodia
- Vietnam

- Rishikesh on the Ganges, where the Beatles went
- Shangri-La

Portuguese authors:
- Carvalho, *A God Strolling in the Cool of the Evening*
- Saramago, many books
- António Antunes

Travel writer:
- Pico Iyer

Books:
- *Never Let Me Go*
- *Survival in Auschwitz*

Good sites for lectures:
- WikiLectures
- Academic Earth
- TED, awesome stuff

"The Window"

The window is so small
. . . and it's closing.
Give me the road
Give me the vagabond spirits,
the restless souls
wandering the streets of life
in search of nothing
. . . and everything.

{113}

There is nothing I want more than to meet a girl and get a hotel room for three days. I had one, but I ruined it with the truth. Lesson learned.

Don't give me your judgment, you slut. You know that's what people would call you. Fuck your objective morality. I'm not hurting anyone or at least not you.

"Gratification"

To all the women who have been nice enough to touch me,

Thank you.

{114}

I think I drank some bad water on the Baltic Sea ferry, and now my stomach won't leave me alone.

Is there anyone who doesn't snore, terrorizing hostels across the land?

In the sobriety of morning, Mari didn't want me anymore.

Prague, what do you hold for me? Will I look back upon you fondly? I'm addicted to the unknown.

Tell me what you want from me, and I will let you know if I can provide it.

Esoteric references.

Sometimes I wonder if I am lost.

It's a shocking feeling when you're found out. I really don't like lying, but anonymity is important. I didn't count on actually hanging out with someone for so long, especially a Harvard PhD like Mark. He's much more observant than the average person. What does this mean? Is Allan Sparks dead? Is Tyler Durden dead? I feel bad but whatever, you know. I kind of want to run. Yeah I am a "sketchy motherfucker." I suck. My first reaction is to drink. I'm too nice, too involved in conversation to be fake. Do I rename myself?

Can I force myself to love Shelly? Can I ever escape cell phone rings?

Prague is a beautiful, incredible city, but it has so many goddamn tourists.

I close my eyes on a bridge, the sun beats on my face as the sounds from a saxophone fill the air, and thousands of people pass by the locals selling their wares. "Draw you a portrait? Jewelry?"

Girls in short skirts toying with man's imagination.

There are billions of stars in a galaxy, and there are billions of galaxies. The vastness of the universe is incomprehensible. I do not believe in God, and yet I cannot imagine a more mysterious existence than being a human being on planet Earth. Our thoughts, brains, and evolutionary path are so improbable.

Discussions on falling in love: you can't plan it; you can't run from it; you can't predict it; you just wake up, and it's there.

Is thirty really the new twenty? Has our increased lifespan changed when we do things?

A Kiwi girl is staying in our dorm room. I had forgotten how funny the Kiwi accent is, the way they say "like" or when they end a sentence with the word "like"—"We went out to the bars and it was so fun like. We were all in hysterics."

"Random"

Pseudo bit hydroxide,
Forrest et al petrified,
Dignified,
Stone martyrs.

But what have you done lately?
Lately?
Lately I've done nothing.

{115}

This morning I think I caught the Kiwi girl staring at me with curious, lust-filled eyes.

Mark and I spent over three hours this afternoon at a deserted café discussing the art of writing. Then we went to St. Vitus Cathedral.

"Old Churches"

Gargoyle ferocity
Francilien verbosity
Conquistadorian vengeance
Odious glances
Threatening stances
Beastly extravagance
Oedipalian significance
Stainless dreams
and Presbyterian hopes

{116}

I used to somewhat yearn to hear an American accent. Now I long to get away from it.

"Virality"

English, English, everywhere,
Not a culture to spare.

{117}

Prague is simply breathtaking. I've seen beautiful cities before but never on this scale. It's like the Magic Kingdom, except real.

As Mark and I made our way towards the Old Town Square on our nightly quest for girls, my ears picked up the faint sound of music emanating from a small side-street pub. It was clearly a local dive, and Mark wanted to keep going since the prospect of girls would be small.

We stopped on the sidewalk and debated for a minute or two. I have always valued the overall travel experience above simply chasing women, and the chance to hear live Czech music was too good to pass up. Eventually I convinced him to go in for a drink.

Inside there were only two other patrons. A man with unkempt facial hair and missing teeth sat next to a woman that stared at us an inordinate amount of time. Her eyes followed us to our seats like a dog follows the serving of a freshly cooked steak.

The source of the music was an old man sitting behind a long wooden table playing acoustic guitar. He didn't acknowledge our presence. He just kept right on singing with unabated passion, and despite Mark being quadrilingual, neither of us had any idea what the song was about. However, it was clear we had stumbled upon something unique.

Our senses were quickly overwhelmed as we took in our surroundings. The man behind the table was dressed in the strangest amalgamation. He wore what appeared to be an old soldier's uniform with combat-style boots laced so tightly that his leg would sooner break off than he'd roll an ankle. A leather cowboy hat sat confidently on his head with a Confederate flag sewn to the front. Next to him was a beat-up backpack covered by a beautiful, bluish-green shawl that he carefully lifted whenever he accessed his bag.

He played relentlessly, only pausing briefly between songs to take another giant swig of beer and to occasionally shake his glass at the bartender when he needed more. The bartender looked like Sam Malone except better. He wore a plain white T-shirt under a button down and had only bothered to fasten the bottom two buttons. For him it appeared to be just another night as he lazily read the paper while the madman soldier cowboy sang his heart out four feet away.

Mark and I were mesmerized by the whole scene. There were so many questions we wanted to ask. Our curiosity and apprehension increased when the guitar player rose to go to the bathroom. An eight-inch bowie knife hung menacingly from his side while a patch of the state of Oklahoma was sewn to his back right pocket. Was he a fan of the Old West, the South, or rebellion in general?

When he returned, he carefully lifted the shawl and pulled a tattered notebook from his pack. As he diligently flipped through it, Mark elbowed me. "Those are his songs," he whispered. I leaned forward in my seat and strained my neck to get a glimpse. Each page contained one or more stanzas with various pictures beside them; some looked to be cut from magazines.

Eventually he stopped at a page and studied it for a moment before putting the notebook away. Then he broke into a rhythm I had never quite heard before; it was soft but aggressive, erratic but steady. My hands and feet took on a life of their own as they moved inexorably to the music. I glanced at Mark, and he was doing the same. He saw me look over and held up his glass to cheers mine, thanking me with his eyes for the unforgettable experience.

The Czech cowboy played on like this with such an unbridled passion as if he could resurrect past lovers. He had to have been at least sixty years old, and his face was weathered with a harsh life, yet his body and spirit were strong.

He took no breaks other than to relieve himself from the constant flow of alcohol. He sang and yelled and picked and strummed with seemingly endless energy.

Later in the evening, a fat balding man sauntered into the bar and sat next to the cowboy. His shirt had stains, and he wore dark navy sweatpants. He looked homeless. The cowboy paid him no mind until after a few songs he held the guitar towards him, offering a chance to play. The balding man looked at it for a moment before accepting. Mark and I were immediately concerned we had heard the last from the cowboy.

The man's fingers were so plump it seemed like they might not fit between the frets. He strummed the strings a few times with his thumb and soon became comfortable with the instrument. He continued playing and began to sing with a gentleness and beauty that belied all appearance. Operatic in nature his voice filled the bar in such a way that even Sam Malone looked up from his paper. Mark and I stared in disbelief. This guy should have been filling concert halls; instead, he was in a sketchy bar singing for six people.

The writers in us could only wonder what he was doing there. Was he classically trained, or was he born with this gift? Did he try to become famous until he had some horrible fall from grace? An addiction perhaps? Or did he consciously choose to turn down a life entertaining rich people in tuxedos? Hell, for all we knew he was famous; we wouldn't have recognized him; we couldn't even understand the words he was singing. But we knew they were beautiful.

After the song he handed the guitar back to the cowboy who nodded his approval and slid his drink over, saying something in Czech. The fat man reached for the beer when suddenly the carnie-looking patron jumped out of his seat speaking emphatically. We weren't sure what was happening until the bartender calmly set down his paper and began to fill three glasses.

Meanwhile, the girl was making ever stronger eyes at Mark. Perhaps she was a prostitute, or maybe she just found his dark skin tone exotic; either way, he couldn't take it anymore and moved to my side of the table so he wouldn't have to look at her.

The three men toasted their glasses high in the air, and the cowboy polished his off like he had been stranded in the desert for days. The scraggly patron said something as he pointed at the bartender and then the glass, and the bartender refilled it. The cowboy smiled in appreciation before drinking half the glass in a single gulp. Then he grabbed his guitar and broke into a ballad.

The highs and lows of his voice spoke true as he demonstrated his musical range. The fat man had talent no doubt, but the cowboy had an aura, an authenticity that can't be taught or faked. It can only come from life experience and the realities of a complex soul. "He's . . . marvelous," Mark muttered in enchantment.

Midway through the second chorus the fat man joined in as if they had rehearsed the song a thousand times. As far as we could tell they had just met, and yet their voices harmonized perfectly like they had been specially chosen to serenade the stars. And it felt like dreaming when they did a call and response over an improvised bridge.

When the song was over, the cowboy quickly finished his drink. Then he tapped it twice on the table to indicate he wanted more. While the bartender obliged, the gap-toothed man said something, and the cowboy stood to respond. We had no idea what they were talking about, but the cowboy became increasingly agitated, waving his arms and pounding the table. His face grew red as his speech got faster and louder. Mark and I eyed his knife pensively. We were concerned the situation was about to escalate, and we were pretty far from the door.

The bartender set a full glass on the table, and the cowboy talked for another heated minute before picking it up and holding it out in an imaginary toast. Then he downed it, and we were relieved to see a smile cross his face. We'll never be sure whether he was actually angry, telling a joke, doing an impersonation, or stating an impassioned political position.

Sitting back down, he began to play with a renewed energy and anger in total contrast to the previous song. He hit the strings with such velocity I thought all six might break at once. But the guitar was an extension of his own body, and he knew what it could handle.

The fat man stood for the first time and leaned over to speak to the bartender who promptly handed him two spoons. He listened to the rhythm for a moment and then added silverware accompaniment. The cowboy fed off the new sound and wailed even harder.

He kept on like this, playing more songs and drinking more beer until his motor skills began to wane, and his behavior became increasingly erratic. At one point he reached for his glass and grabbed a fistful of air two inches to the right. When he finally got it to his lips, he spilled half of it down his soldier's coat only to look up laughing like a common rummy.

"Let's go," Mark said. "I don't want to see him like this. I want to remember him for what we was. Let's leave before it gets sad."

"No man," I responded, "let's stay to see it get real." But Mark really wanted to go, and I didn't want to risk marring his memory of the experience, so I acquiesced.

On our way out we thanked the cowboy, and he nodded towards the table. Mark and I stopped, wondering if we were supposed to leave a tip. Sensing our confusion, the man with the scraggly facial hair explained in a heavy accent of broken English, "He plays for drinks."

I turned to the bartender, but Mark was already on it. "Three whiskeys."

"Whiskey," the cowboy said slowly in awe. As far as we could tell it was the only English word he knew.

Hearing Mark's voice, the scraggly man asked, "Where you from?"

"The States," I answered. Almost instantly the cowboy sprang from his seat and pointed at the Oklahoma patch on his back right pocket. Then he lifted his hat and looked at the Confederate flag in the front like he was verifying it was still there before showing it to me proudly. I wanted to ask him so many questions, not just about his clothes, but about everything, from his philosophy on life, to his childhood, to how he first learned guitar. But he wouldn't have understood me, not without a translator, and soon Mark handed us each a whiskey. We toasted happily, and then in a few seconds the sound of three glasses hit the table.

We reentered the night somewhat dazed at what we had just experienced but soon remembered our original mission and headed towards the town square.

{118}

A Spanish goddess floats around the dance floor. Mark calls her "The Muse." Everything about her is perfect as if she were the product of male focus groups. What is the sexiest way for a woman to smoke a cigarette?

We use words like esoteric, which is itself esoteric.

Ostentatious calumny.

Gucci makes me want to vomit.

On the ferry to Russia, I met a Colombian beauty. She was traveling with a group, which was unfortunate because I think she might have slept with me otherwise.

The pleasure of memories, *voluptas memorias*.

"Bohemian Angel"

Flowing skirt
Tan skin
Dark hair
Handful of flowers.
Bare feet on cobblestone
in some forgotten alley,
an archway to your heart.
Her head is turned, but you can tell she's smiling.
It's so beautiful,
you're happy for her,
even though you don't know her.

{119}

Steve Jobs died today. You changed the world. Thank you. Why did you have to go so soon? What else could you have done? What else would you have done? Dreamer, thinker, doer. If I was going to die today, what would I do?

Mari was so cold to me at the end. I think she was being someone else. What if I had asked her about going to India the first night we hung out? What would she have said then?

Prague is really beautiful, but I don't like it or at least not its people. It reminds me of Zurich as far as the nightlife, and I don't particularly want to spend another day here.

I need to look my wife in the eyes and see what I feel. I love her, but do you stay with someone for the past? The sex is lacking. The sex life is good, but the sex itself isn't there.

I'm living in two worlds and developing a vast network. The problem is they can't meet, and so the network is smaller.

And the last layer of the onion is peeled away.

Will anyone ever refer to me as an intellectual giant?

I'm already thinking about my next trip.

Tonight I toasted to Steve Jobs with a girl from New Zealand in a Prague pub.

{120}

And just like that, you're alone, and it's glorious, at least for now. Leaving another hostel, that revolving door of backpackers. Racing to beat checkout. You meet people, hang out for a day or two, and then you move on, probably to never see each other again. Is there some grand, predestined purpose to a chance meeting? Almost certainly not.

While I waited for my train out of town, I went to Burger King. It's kind of sad, you know, the Americanization of everything, but I couldn't stand to give Prague any more of my money. I'm so jaded on this city.

When you're with a new woman, there's the excitement of the unknown, looking for a sign, a brush of a hand, legs touching, something to let you know it's okay to advance.

I wanted inside her. I wanted to hold her feet by the ankles and give her all I had. In the end though, I just didn't click with the New Zealand girl. We had a lot in common, but that's the way it goes—sometimes you have little in common and you click, other times you have much in common and don't.

Potential title: *The Prose Diary*

Goddamn, I need a new pen. I've been using a fucking pencil the last few days. My previous pen ran dry, and I'm pretty sure Justin took my other one.

Do you stay in a relationship out of loyalty or out of love?

I feel nothing. I am numb. I care for nothing but the road. Is the road real, or is it just people pretending? Whatever happens, whatever goes wrong, I rest soundly knowing the road is out there.

I've been eating like shit! Absolute shit! After feeling so skinny for the first part of the trip, I acclimated to travel, and now I'm eating regularly, which typically means fast food. Now I feel fat, fucking fat.

And once again, self-loathing creeps in.

The pain in my heart hurts like a puncture wound. Life, loss, opportunities I will never have again. Epoch events missed, always wondering what they must have been like with a touch of regret. Has it all been worth it?

I want to suck the marrow out of the bones of life.

I think it's better to go to a place where you're exotic. Fuck Prague. I'd rather be on the edges. I'd rather be a dove than a pigeon.

I really need a new pen!

"Missing Muse"

Woe is muse,
where are you?
I need you,
your inspiration.
We could be on the trail,
me following you with my pen,
you just being you—
your voice, your laugh, your thighs.
Woe is muse,
where are you?

{121}

I meet so many girls and nothing happens; then I meet Mari and completely fall for her. If I hadn't told her the truth, I could've had her.

There is much more time to think and observe when you're by yourself. Also, I write a lot more when I'm alone.

In future trips, I want to eat better—fruits and vegetables, not fucking fast food and street vendors.

This trip may have changed my life in ways that aren't entirely clear. I want to be the skinny backpacker, the rail-thin backpacker.

Maybe, quite possibly, I live for the road. It's not what I do but who I am.

The Czech cowboy gets by on his charm . . . his charm and his rhythm.

Sometimes I feel that I've used Shelly like a parasite, and I wish there was a way I could make it right. I wish I could give her millions of dollars to make up for me.

Shelly's job allows us to live anywhere in the US, but it's not enough.

You cannot blame me for all that I have done, but you should.

I want to cry because I think my mind might be hanging by a thread, my torn soul.

I am genuinely nice but have developed the ability or channeled an innate ability to be absolutely vicious and ruthless when I feel threatened. It's probably evolutionary.

It seems like people are constantly in my way.

A girl on the road says she left home to escape small-mindedness and judgment, but then when discussing another girl at our hostel she begins a sentence with, "What kind of self-respecting female..."

I am confused by all of this.

I love being on an empty train car with a notebook.

Passing through Bavaria gives me a warm feeling: chopped wood, green country, cute little houses.

When you've been traveling in non-English speaking countries for a while, it becomes weird to talk to people again and know they will understand you. You can use all your colloquialisms and talk as fast as you want.

After dealing with the rudeness of Prague, I'm questioning whether Shelly and I should go to France. Maybe we should go to Spain instead where the people will probably be much nicer.

Unconsummated desire haunts me like an ambivalent glance. I can only wonder what it means, what she would have been like. I swear, in another situation, me and that Colombian...

I can't decide how I feel about the Starbucksification of everything. I guess most of the time I don't like it.

"The Passenger Train"

Beautiful countryside,
thick forests,
scattered hillside houses,
horses grazing.
Solitary railroad tracks
weaving through forgotten towns
where people live and die.

{122}

"The Czech Cowboy"

He made the whole trip worth it,
Adjustable, loveable muse.
He gets by on his charm,
his charm and his rhythm.

Ambiguously belligerent,
Townes Van Zandt incarnate.

His demons are put to rest through song,
through song and hard drink.

You cannot know him,
only enjoy him.
Somewhere in my heart,
I will always be searching for the Czech Cowboy.

{123}

And suddenly I am comfortable alone, confident, like a bird who has finally learned to fly.

"A Beckoning"

The road constantly beckons.
I hear a song and the road beckons
I read a poem and the road beckons
I see a photograph and the road beckons
I watch a movie and the road beckons
I close my eyes and the road beckons
I fall asleep and the road beckons
I wake up and the road beckons . . .

{124}

Everyone wants to go where they are liked.

I have seen old friends and made several new ones on this trip—Reko, Mark, soon Tara. My social network is spreading vastly.

I've had deep conversations with a lot of people. It seems like I've met someone new everyday. I've also gathered knowledge and culture from the road. Books, music, websites, lectures.

What's my next trip? A solo visit to Portugal, Asia—alone or with Justin? Amsterdam with Shelly? France? Spain?

Will you make us both come while we hold hands?

I need to exercise; I have not moved faster than a walk in about seven weeks.

I've seen quite a few Kindles on this trip. A touchscreen Kindle would be so much better and faster.

If I could make $40,000 a year from something creative, I would be the happiest person in the world.

"American soldiers carry their guns as if they're ready to use them." Or so I've heard.

A girl keeps looking at me; can I go hit on her?

I would travel to the ends of the earth to find the right adjective.

A Kiwi accent using Irish words—disappointing.

I suppose I should read about the next city I'll be visiting . . .

Girls with neck tattoos, am I done with you?

It is so hard for me to say no to a woman.

"I'm glad you were honest with me, Allan."

The callous around my heart bleeds deep but heals quickly.

Part of me doesn't want my home; it just wants my backpack and really it doesn't even care about that, just my journals and my books, and those just need to be digitized, and then I need nothing.

College football, the World Series, you don't pay any attention to these things when you're on the road.

Am I simple? No, I'm complicated.

Can one person alone fill the hole in my soul?

Everywhere I look, people are committing suicide with nicotine.

The industrial smokestacks are beautiful in a weird way.

I've been on so many ferries and trains this trip, including three night trains and four night ferries. Then it's been hostel, hostel, hostel.

I want to remain a mystery on the road.

And now I'm off to see an old friend, to share a bottle of wine.

My heart screams for freedom.

Maybe I should write a poem called "The Heart" and include any references I've made to the heart on this trip.

So many travelers I've met prefer to travel alone, which is very interesting.

Old German woods flashing by my window, I wonder what they've seen over the last millennia.

"Ululation"

This is written for a girl I fell in love with.
For various complicated reasons, it did not work out.

It was mad.
It was passionate.
It was brief.

Do you believe in regret?
In doubt
In guilt?
Yes to the former
No to the latter.
The rain falls,
pitter,
patter.
Do you believe in God
In religion
In love?
The snow falls,
gently, softly
from above.
Do you believe things happen for a reason
The time change
another season?
Do you believe in birth control
and that humans have a soul?
Do you believe in Marx
or Smith?

OPAQUE REFERENCES TO THE BALTIC SEA 141

The answer's in between I guess.
Do you believe in heroes and demons
In categories and division
In strength
In numbers
In hope
and loss
In obituaries
and the Holocaust
In righteousness
and sacrilege
In Oedipal
and patronage?
Do you believe in something
In nothing
In anything
In tests
and questions
and answers
In power
In dreams
In dreams coming true
In earthquakes
and paradise
In ambiguity
and people being nice
In basketball
and clothes
In drugs
and dust up your nose
Injections
and needles
and pills

America
abortion
and wills
In trains
and automobiles
In strangers
and lust
In cannabis
In fame
fortune
and desire
Light and bombs
cast upon
funeral pyres
In the moon
stars
Earth
ellipses
In culture
and preservation of language
or homogenization
and anglicization
of tribes, warriors and traditions
In streets
and pavement
In roads
and bridges
In nationalities
In the UN and EU and OPEC?
Do you realize all of this,
all of Earth is just a speck?
On a cosmic Milky Way,
one of billions of billions,

half a grain of sand on an endless beach?
Do you believe in madness, gladness and sadness
Fear, riches and glory
Sacred females
and vagrant criminals
Nervous sisters
and horny brothers
Whistles and fists
Condoms
and broken wrists
Ninjas and night
Pregnancy
and what's right
Gypsies and villains
Wives and husbands
Grace
Race
Saving face
Time
Dishonor
Shame
and nuance
In collections
and backpacking
Loneliness and freedom
Catapults and war
In keeping score
In flags
and mercenaries
The pen or the sword
The asylum or the ward
David or Goliath?
Do you believe in victims or responsibility?

In black or white or gray?
Do you pray?
Have you ever?
Would you, if you were on a plane that was going down?
If you wanted to make someone love you?
Or cure a disease?
Do you believe in symbols and lanterns
In drums and patterns
In courage
In music and song
and trying to belong
In old towns full of tourists
In beaches full of nudists
In this
That
and the other
In prodigies
and manatees
Evolution
and confusion
Dogs
Bark
Trees
Thank you
and saying please
In simplification
Miscegenation
and the Aryan Nations
In ghosts, goblins and ghouls
In fools
In paragraphs, chapters and books
In fire, lightning and crooks
In presidents and congressmen

In reincarnation
In virgins
In heaven
In worm food
Coen brothers
and The Dude
Movies, film and arithmetic
The monkey
and the stick
The opposable thumb
Bipedal to run
Moses and the commandments
Allah
and Sharia law
Militants
and acrobats
Gymnasts
and sycophants
Definitions
Abbreviations
Obligations
Notoriety
Deuteronomy
Taxonomy
The sacred and the profane
The gifted and the damned
The woman and the man
Watches and clocks
Buying stocks
Hostels, hotels, apartments, condos
Never, sometimes, always, maybe
Holidays
Turkey, gravy

Football
American and otherwise
That you're better than the other guys
Double crosses and traps
Oligopoly and aristocrats
Or egalitarianism
Contrarianism and mischievism
In Champagne and sparkling wine
Homeless loners
Cunts and boners
Rags to riches
Prisoners in ditches
Wind and sleet
Chance
and all the people you meet
Mothers, fathers, sons and daughters
The captain and the crew
All the things you thought you knew
In Titus and the gods
In Jobs
Work
and Gates
Blocking access
Granting access
All that Woz
and all that could've been
In a lover and a friend
In the beginning
and the end?

{125}

People on the road are generally areligious and volunteer that information readily.

The women in Nürnberg are fucking beautiful.

My grandmother passed away while I was traveling, and I didn't go to her funeral. I think part of me will always regret that. Of all the times for her to pass away . . . I hadn't seen her for six years. What the fuck? She wouldn't have known who I was anyway though.

I wonder where my aunt was when my grandmother died since my dad was trying to buy my grandmother's house at the time.

My grandmother was German. I'm in Germany. I should try to honor her in some way or reflect on her or write a poem for her, "Dear Grandma." I'll go to a quiet place and write "Dear Grandma," maybe in the Tiergarten. I'd do it now, but I'm too hungry and tired. Besides, I'd rather let nature inspire it.

I don't want your products or your lies.

When I hurt—*High Violet*

Maybe I'll write something for Steve Jobs, a song or a poem.

I kind of feel like that New Zealand girl was a little bit of a fraud, but maybe so am I, maybe we all are.

I still have visions of that cute Polish girl.

I wanted to kill that Irishman. I still want to kill him. Thank god I hadn't had any whiskey that night.

I have to be careful; I feel depression coming on.

<u>Song about a racist Irishman</u>:

"Walk Away"

(Instrumental should be heavy, especially at the chorus)

<u>First Verse</u> (meter similar to a children's nursery rhyme)

This song
Is the only way
I can stop from killing you
Fuck you
You racist prick
You can suck my fuckin' dick

For your racist talk
Make you a bloody mess
On the sidewalk
Guinness guts and Jameson brains
Everywhere
Everywhere

<u>Chorus</u> (screamed)

FUCK YOU
YOU RACIST PRICK
YOU CAN SUCK MY FUCKIN' DICK
NOW
SHUT UP AND WALK AWAY
SHUT UP AND WALK AWAY

WHY DON'T YOU JUST
SHUT UP AND WALK AWAY

Second Verse

The discriminated
has become
the discriminator
A fucking hater
Well if you want hate
I won't hesitate

Bridge (over a mix of Irish/carnival sounding music)

I took a shit
Out came a racist mick
I don't need a stick
to beat your ass
I'll do it with my fists
Cracking bone against knuckles
Cracking bone against knuckles

Back to Verse

How does it feel
Hated no reason why
You need not apply
I will make you die

Chorus (screamed)

FUCK YOU
YOU RACIST PRICK
YOU CAN SUCK MY FUCKIN' DICK
NOW

SHUT UP AND WALK AWAY
SHUT UP AND WALK AWAY
WHY DON'T YOU JUST
SHUT UP AND WALK AWAY

<u>Third Verse</u>

You say you went to school
but you're a fuckin' fool
Educated ignorance
Culture of miscreants

Fuck you
You racist prick
You make me sick
Accent like a mouth full of shit
I won't hate your country
But I will hate you
YOU

<u>Chorus</u> (screamed)

FUCK YOU
YOU RACIST PRICK
YOU CAN SUCK MY FUCKIN' DICK
NOW
SHUT UP AND WALK AWAY
SHUT UP AND WALK AWAY
WHY DON'T YOU JUST
SHUT UP AND WALK AWAY

<u>Fourth Verse</u>

Don't test your luck
You filthy fuck

Stay home
I'm sure there's a gutter all alone
that misses you

Your fake apology
doesn't fool me
You're just a bigot
A bigot
A MOTHERFUCKING BIGOT

<u>Chorus</u> (screamed)

FUCK YOU
YOU RACIST PRICK
YOU CAN SUCK MY FUCKIN' DICK
NOW
SHUT UP AND WALK AWAY
SHUT UP AND WALK AWAY
WHY DON'T YOU JUST
SHUT UP AND WALK AWAY

(crescendo into an instrumental on the verge of out of control, then end with no music screaming the following)

<u>End</u> (somewhat fade out on the last line)

SHUT UP AND WALK AWAY
SHUT UP AND WALK AWAY
FUCK YOU
YOU RACIST PRICK
SHUT UP AND WALK AWAY

{126}

I might be borderline psychotic.

I've become insatiable.

I feel bad for what I don't feel.

Bigger, badder, more. I've become addicted to the rush, the feeling of momentary invincibility.

I think I'm ready for a solo trip.

I have a sense that I should spend some time with my father.

My heart bursts for the road. Maybe I can buy another year or two of travel before having kids.

No one can know where I am. Just me. I feel intensely happy right now, being on this train, alone, anonymous; no one could find me even if they wanted to. I feel like a bird floating on shifting winds.

Every time I leave, I get the sense that Shelly wonders if I will return, if this will be the time I don't come back. I guess I want to work on our relationship, assuming there is a way to make it work.

I feel like the whole second half of my life, or at least the last ten years, has been building towards who I became on this trip. I'm pretty sure I have changed or perhaps finally realized who I really am.

Maybe I'm outwardly simple, but my depths are complicated. I am leading two lives.

I hate when the train stops moving; it's like meditation interrupted.

I could talk for days about what has happened on this trip. But Shelly is the only person I could tell it all to, and she said she doesn't want to hear about it, which is why I guess I'll tell it to a piece of paper or a computer screen.

I wish I had taken a photo of that poster Mark and I saw in Prague, the one of the beautiful barefoot woman holding flowers in an alley. Maybe I can find it online.

I can't believe how much I'm writing. This has never happened before, not like this.

I am regularly discussing art and literature with graduates of Harvard and Yale. I have climbed the ladder rung by rung with my brain. Amazing.

At her flat in Bamberg, Tara and I stayed up late into the night drinking wine and discussing calloused hearts, philosophy, love, and anger.

Sometimes I feel like a photographer traveling the world for that perfect shot.

"The Traveler"

A smoker lights a cigarette,
inhaling to forget.
Sorrow and loss,
Nicotine addiction,
Wishing his life was fiction.
He blows smoke into the air,
pretending he doesn't care,

about life,
a wife,
the way he looks,
or reading books.
He ponders woe is me,
as if anything mattered,
recalling the barista he flattered,
hopes of a quick lay.
But today
he's waiting for a train
to take him to another city.
While he contemplates this pity,
the tension in his loins,
and the naked body he will never see,
there's a roar up the tracks,
a single light in the dusk.
He takes one last drag
tosses the fag
grabs his bag
like he's done a thousand times before,
and steps through the open door.
Another beginning has come to an end,
and he's on the road again.

{127}

It seems I write best or most inspired when I'm alone on a moving train. I write for hours and hours without thought, in a meditative zone, surrendering myself to my pen. No one looks twice at me, and I love it. Right now the words come faster than my pen can move, and it's almost exhausting. When I try to put my notebook away another idea comes to me before I can close my bag, and I have to take it out again. Will there be a day when the words no longer come at all?

The girl we met in Copenhagen is the type of woman who knows exactly what she wants and exactly how to get it—the modern day equivalent of a railroad tycoon. She will never be satisfied.

On my way to another city, whom will I fuck? Anyone? Someone? No one?

I have no idea what I'll discover in Berlin. Maybe I won't even talk to anyone for three days. Who knows? I feel like I'm traveling to Mecca. The word on the road is Berlin. The pulse of the artists is Berlin. 1920s Paris, 1950s New York, 1960s San Francisco, Berlin in the 2010s. At what point will it all be ruined—one year, two years, or is it already?

Bavarian houses with neatly stacked wood flash by my train window.

We had nothing in common, but we had everything in common—Americans.

I had no idea what he was saying, but I understood exactly what he meant.

Transfer to train ICE 1606.

Has my wife become like a mistress? Can she accept this lifestyle? That it's not a passing phase?

I have a sense that what I'm doing is greatness, even if the greatness is only for me and my individual life, and that's why I can't stop.

I kind of want to do whatever will trigger passion.

The ignominious man. The mad poet, writer, scientist. The gypsy, physician, paramedic.

A trust fund gone awry and a large white pillow pressed against an old woman's face.

{128}

"Dear Grandma"

Dear Grandma,

I'm sorry I missed your funeral. Shoot, I'm sorry I haven't visited for six years. I wonder if you would have recognized me, the Alzheimer's, you know.

If you could know me, would you be proud of me? Were you ever?

Growing up, I remember that visiting you was like an interview with a collegiate admissions officer. I nervously hoped I was saying the right things to make you like me.

Were you happy with your life? Are you happy it's over? You'd been through so much: the cancer and the Alzheimer's, the diabetes and the dentures, the car accident and the paralysis.

Your father died when you were thirteen; pardon my language, but did that fuck you up?

Do you think your resultant unearned wealth affected your spiritual growth? Do you care? Did you ever? Did it make you mistrust the motivations of others, including your own children? Or did you like the power it gave you?

I know you enjoyed chess. I remember you and my father playing often. I wish I had been old enough to play when you were still of sound mind.

Did you ever play chess with people's lives?

Did you believe in God? Or were your donations just for social status?

Were you racist? Did you vote for Kennedy or Nixon?

How did you celebrate the end of World War II?

Did you get drunk?

Did you ever get drunk?

Did you ever get drunk and black out?

What is your biggest secret and why? Did you ever cheat on Grandpa? Did he ever cheat on you?

If you had one more healthy day, how would you spend it? I'm saying you can walk again and everything. Would you hike up a mountain and play chess at the top and then cry when the day was over?

What kind of music did you like? Did you curse the Beatles while secretly tapping your foot?

I understand you were 100 percent German. Did you ever visit the Fatherland? If not, did you ever want to?

You liked horses. Why?

Were you capable of love or only calculation?

Did you want to fuck up your kids, or was it an accident?

Did you ever have an abortion?

Were you brave enough to answer these questions? Maybe to an anonymous stranger, on the road, under a pseudonym?

Your blood pumps in me, you know. Your genes have been passed on. Your answers could help me. How did you deal with anger? Revenge? Depression? Lust? Could you control them? Or channel them? Or hide them?

I wish I could know your life philosophy. On New York City subway cars you encouraged your children to talk to strangers. What made you think of doing that?

Was it for amusement, or was it the strategy of a wise mother bird teaching her chicks to fly on their own?

You should know the art of talking to strangers has been passed on to me, at least by example. And I will consciously pass it on to my kids. Was this by design? Did you think that many moves ahead?

Did your German dreams come true, or did you settle?

What was your favorite book? Movie? Album?

Possessions seemed important to you. If you could take one thing with you, what would it be?

If you could put one item in the Smithsonian, what would it be and why?

Did you ever wake up in the night wishing you had worn your seat belt?

Were you aware of all the circling vultures at the end of your life, the people moving in to eat the remains of your estate? Did you care? Or did you just like the attention?

If you could give me one piece of advice, what would it be?

I hope you are happy now or at least not hurting anymore. I wish I could say you are walking in meadows holding hands with Grandpa, but we both know that's probably not true.

Almost undoubtedly I will join you someday, but we will never meet again. I guess that's what gives life so much value.

Your grandson

{129}

I figure we are heading towards one world government or at least one nation. I don't think it will happen easily. First there will probably be a nuclear war, most likely involving the United States. The result will be so horrific that people will support an end to national divisions.

You might hate me, and I might feel bad, but I will have all this joy and pleasure in the meantime. And so it is, that once again, I become Allan Sparks.

Why do some people turn newspaper and magazine pages so violently? It's really annoying.

I need to watch *Schindler's List*.

You can take my coat and my bag, but please don't take my passport and notebooks, especially my notebooks.

I want to be buried with an open notebook and a pen between my fingers.

I haven't felt so content in years as I do riding the train by myself.

Will I have clairvoyant tranquility when I return home, or will I go right back to the American grind?

My only pair of jeans is completely tattered. The base of the right pant leg got caught in the spoke of a bicycle in Bamberg and is now held together by a safety pin. There's a growing hole in the middle of the crotch area that has somehow managed to stay hidden. It has become a goal, a challenge, to make them last the rest of the trip.

I'm considering going to visit my family for Thanksgiving or maybe going to my extended family's Christmas celebration.

I can't remember if I emailed my brother about being able to help with his wedding.

Are leather pants back in style?

Am I a traveler, or am I pretending? Maybe Iowa is who I am, and this is just something I do. An Iowa Christmas when I'm forty with snow and my own family would be nice. Am I trying to regain something I've already lost and can't get back? Are my travels all a fool's errand? Then who is Mark? What about Mark? Does it matter? Is this only a passing moment of doubt? Is the doubt real?

Germanic precision and efficiency are matched only by American ingenuity and motivation.

The train is stopping at the Leipzig station. It looks the same as it did when I was here three years ago. On that trip, I met a girl who was fighting insurmountable sexual desire, especially for American men. "I will do anything for Americans," she had said lustfully.

I wish the train conductor wouldn't repeat everything in English. But I guess they don't use English for the English; they use it for the Swedes, the Finns, the Brazilians, and everyone else who doesn't speak the local language. It's only natural there would be a default international language. And I suppose I'm lucky it happens to be my native tongue.

I take a nap, and my lust returns. I've had three orgasms at the hands of other women on this trip, and it's been wonderful.

A girl across from me has a cute silver earring in the shape of a star. It reminds me of one of those child reward stickers.

Tara told me I hadn't changed since she saw me eight years ago, and I was disappointed. What the hell has everything been for if I'm still the same?

"How long did you go to college for?"

"Seven years. It was soul crushing."

Leave me alone. I so want to quit Facebook. Everything disappears like a napalm canister of dreams.

I listen to the word of the road like a kid with his ear on the railroad tracks. The heartbeat throbs Berlin. The nomadic vagabonds whisper Berlin. Everyone talks of moving there—Mari, Mark, the guy on the couch in St. Petersburg. All the drama will continue in America while I obliviously write in Berlin. The energy, the magic, has Berlin learned from San Francisco? It will eventually be ruined as it must be, and in ten to fifteen years it will happen somewhere else. But knowing it won't last makes it all the more valuable.

I am completely ignored in Europe, and I love it. No one looks twice at me writing or even once for that matter.

I am planning to take a night train from Berlin to the airport in Zurich where I will take a flight to Dulles where I will get on a bus to the metro.

Even though it's daylight, the moon is shining bright in the distance, the same color as the clouds.

Does a cow know when he's eaten his last blade of grass?

My mind intermittently floats to America, the country I know so well.

Nuclear war seems inevitable. What's to stop Russia from launching a nuke from China? Could you imagine being abroad and hearing the words "America is gone"? It gives me chills.

Mark told me all countries are racist, but America is the only one that aspires not to be.

We pass a railway platform where a young couple is holding hands.

I know a girl who was an accountant in the US but moved to Thailand where she became a nocturnal punk rocker.

The railway car to Berlin has become increasingly crowded. We're only twenty-five minutes from the city, and it's nothing but farmland.

I'll tell you if you want to listen, but I don't care if you don't want to hear.

Am I using hyperbolic language to describe people and places that I imagine to be more important than they are?

Mark said he wanted to know war. I reminded him you can't have life experiences if you're not alive.

An old man sits beside me on the train with a thermos of hot chocolate and a fresh package of cookies as if he just stepped out of a Werther's commercial.

Will I drain another pen before all this is done?

Part of me has not given up on Mari, and I imagine us consummating our love several years from now. *If you said the word, I would follow you.*

An American soldier stationed in Bamberg told me, "Men have two emotions: silence and rage."

The world is speeding by my train window.

Is all this just kindergarten poetics?

{130}

"Anticipation"

I was ripped off in Zurich
I got high in Amsterdam
Then again in Copenhagen
I felt bored in Stockholm
I got drunk on the Baltic Sea
I fell in love in Helsinki
I was a trophy in Tallinn
I was a tourist in St. Petersburg
I danced all night in Krakow
I was hated in Prague
I saw a friend in Bamberg
I . . . in Berlin

{131}

Five minutes from Berlin. Still woods. What?

After hanging out nonstop for three days, Mark and I parted not knowing if or when we'd ever see each other again. "Who knows man, maybe we'll meet again, DC, Berlin, or somewhere on the road."

I should write something about a universal longing for friendship and community.

Finally made it to Berlin. The moon is bright and full as I enter the city. I want to find a high ground and howl at the sphere, channeling my prehistoric roots until my hair stands on end. A proclamation to the system, to the world, "You don't own me." I even have the instinct to find others to join me, a de facto pack.

What if you could stay at the modern equivalent of the Chelsea Hotel when it was in its prime?

Almost every time I pull out my notebook, I imagine people around me thinking, "Just what Berlin needs, another fucking writer."

I'm not sure what I'm creating with all this writing—maybe lots of different projects or a resource for lines.

If I read my writing into the voice memo app on my phone and then email the recording to myself, I basically eliminate all risk of losing my words. My notebooks and writing are the only thing I can't replace, but if they're digitized and preserved in some cloud form, then I can't lose them, and the stress, any stress, evaporates, knowing in a way I am free of possessions.

"Somewhere"

Watching, and waiting.
Somewhere people are dancing,
Somewhere throbbing bass pulsates
through intoxicated bodies.
But I don't know where,
so I am here,
in this square.
Watching, and waiting—
to join them.

{132}

Maybe I'll go to bed early tonight and then wake up early and walk East Berlin.

The five bunks in my hostel room are empty except for mine.

Am I too old for this city? If so, what would youthfulness be good for? To capture something forgotten—too fleeting to appreciate at the time?

I'm going to finish this beer and move on to the next bar. Done.

An intriguing woman is sitting on a sofa in a hipster Berlin bar, a single dreadlock falling across her face.

We have nothing in common, but we have everything in common.

America, I know you. I hear your heartbeat across the ocean. America, I love you, but I had to leave you.

"In Berlin"

I know a guy,
In Berlin,
Who has a wife he calls a girlfriend.
He could have climbed the corporate joke,
Instead he's dying of secondhand smoke,
In Berlin.

{133}

I watched a performer named Robert Rustad Amundsen at an open mic night.

If you had the chance to live in San Francisco in 1967, would you go? If you could live with the Beats in New York, would you? If you lived during the time when Paris was in its prime, wouldn't you go there?

"The Dance"

A woman sits alone at the bar,
Smoking a cigarette,
Waiting for someone to work up the courage.

An introduction and a name.
Can I buy you a drink?

She takes a shot,
and lights another cigarette.
Smoke fills the air,
A hand brushes a leg,
Seductive smile,
Mmm, it's been a while.
Feigned interest,
but only one thing on their mind,
looking for a sign
to leave the bar
get in a car
go somewhere
get what they need
feed
the desire
temper the fire
until
it's back to the bar
to begin
again.

{134}

There is no sleep. There are no schedules—only life.

Someone owns the building where you're getting fucked up. Someone owns the bar where you're spending your money.

My fucking Wi-Fi won't work. I love Europe, but it sometimes pisses me off with its fucking shit inefficiency.

Do I want to be somewhere where I'm unique or some place where I'm just another fuckin' writer?

My god, the Australian accent may be the worst sound in the world.

Guys and girls are going to their rooms together. What the fuck? Why are there so many couples at this hostel—what the fuck?

The bunks in my room are full now, and I'm drinking just to fall asleep. I wanted a beer alone in my room, but I guess that's too much to ask.

Why are there so many couples and twelve-year-olds? What the fuck was I doing when I was twelve?

Goddamn my restless soul.

Fuck it, I'm gonna go back out. I came here to see the night more than the day anyway.

I'm watching a pretty girl play puppet master at a bar. She's got three fucking guys waiting on her every move, another guy wrapped around her finger, and yet a fifth panting at her leg like a puppy.

Is Berlin a false plateau? A pseudo enclave? I've seen several people writing, and I heard Nick Cave at a bar, but the guy playing Nick Cave said the art is mostly mediocre, and he hadn't seen anything good for a while. That's discouraging. He said he came here for music but turned to writing. Hmm, I'm already producing in DC, so what would I gain by coming here?

Justin and I will often sit in a central square and just watch a city happen.

When you're traveling, the road becomes your life.

"Unconsummated Desire"

I thought she was cool,
I thought she was different,
But she was just drunk.

She said she wouldn't judge or care,
But if I hadn't told her
I could've had her legs in the air.

I ruined it,
And now I feel like shit.
I could've had her,
But I was honest,
And I lost her.

I hope she has a good life,
I really do,
But if I had been a liar,
I wouldn't have unconsummated desire.

{135}

Is there a hipster arrogance in Berlin that everything is shit? Maybe the cultural epicenter is still America, or maybe it's online without geolocation.

It's Sunday night, and places are open everywhere. At the open mic night, the artists either had good lyrics or good vocals but not both. Does the Manner Born have both? Possibly. I think we just need to make sure we use our singer's voice effectively.

I don't care so long as I'm writing. I think the two Norwegian guys at the open mic show are in it for the girls. It seemed like an act.

The female puppeteer at that last bar was absurd.

I'm getting tired of hipster shit.

What if Shelly and I choose to share the rest of our lives together? Tara says passion ebbs and flows. Maybe she's right. Hopefully she's right.

{136}

A guy next to me at a café looks like a caricature of a douchey college professor. His espresso and perfectly manicured beard portray the illusion of intellectualism while a strategically placed chain protects his wallet and boosts his street cred.

I'm exploding with joy to know I got to see the Czech Cowboy. I'm also exploding with joy to finally be exploring a city on my own, especially Berlin.

I want to make Mari moan under the Spanish moon.

Writing can take you somewhere else. Time can disappear as if you're in a dream, focused, distracted—until you're interrupted by hunger or some asshole turning the pages of his magazine with the force of a riptide, goddammit.

I love being a mysterious traveler, eating alone. Europeans are amazing in how little they pay attention to those around them. Perhaps centuries of slaughtering each other have taught them to mind their own business.

Maybe I don't need Berlin to write; maybe I need the world. Maybe the road provides the tranquility and stimulation I need.

I love writing in pen instead of typing. I haven't used a pen like this in years and never to write so much. It's beautiful.

I write because I have to, but I worry that some people in Berlin may be writing because they think they're supposed to. Of course, who am I to judge? Who am I at all? I certainly don't know who they are; they may be famous writers for all I know.

Being on the road is a constant experience. Even when you're not meeting people, you're learning about yourself.

If God were real, I'm pretty sure He'd hate me.

Last night I met a girl who had every desirable quality a woman can have except looks—there's got to be a song in there somewhere.

The idea is that a poet has to investigate the intricacies of the heart, or at least that's the excuse I make.

If I keep this up, I won't live past forty.

"I've got three questions for you: Do you have a condom? How hard can you fuck me? How early can you leave in the morning?"

"Yes. As hard as you want. Anytime."

Everyone sells beer in Berlin from convenience stores to street vendors. Any hour, day or night, you can buy a beer wherever you go.

It seems like Berlin is actually kind of small, like you could run into the same people over and over. I saw the Norwegian open mic performers walking down the street in a completely different part of town. Or maybe people just gravitate to various niche communities.

I have to get home to Shelly. It's time. I need to stop drinking like this. Of course I'm sure Shelly and I will have a bottle of wine the first night I'm home. Then the following weekend we'll go to Talladega where we'll drink a bunch more. I swear, it never stops.

I met Nick Cave fans in Berlin. I heard Alela Diane at a café. The cafés are packed with people writing.

When I'm traveling, I find that if a beautiful woman looks at you for longer than a moment, it almost invariably means she's a prostitute. A prostitute's eyes have a particularly vacant stare, a desperate yet indifferent soulless attempt at seduction. Your heart leaps for a moment, thinking the gaze is sincere. Then you realize what she's really after and that there's nothing special about you compared to any other guy with money.

If I write, will more girls want me?

"The Passerby"

He walked by me like a ghost,
sending chills through my soul.
In his wake
roses turn to stone.
His face,
his demeanor,
a paradigm of the sinister.
Thin as a pitchfork
Mean as a trident,
I pretended not to notice him,
and I was glad when he was gone.

{137}

"Why don't you speak German?"

Why don't I speak German? You condescending bitch. You only speak German because of my country's good graces. You should have been wiped off the map, you mass-murdering cunt.

It was one of those situations where you can think of a thousand things to say only after the fact. I was so shocked that it was happening that I wasn't able to respond in the moment.

I had been eating a salad at a café across from my hostel when these two girls started making eyes at me. At first I thought they might be into me, but then I assumed at least one of them was a prostitute. Still, I couldn't resist approaching them to ask if they could recommend any good places to go out.

Eventually they invited me to join them at their table for a beer. The prostitute-looking girl had the most seductive eyes. She also seemed like she might be high on something. The other girl was really nice and sincere. She was born in Turkey but had lived in Berlin most of her life. She had song lyrics from a band called Joy Division tattooed on her forearm.

We made small talk for several minutes. I told them my name was Allan, and I was from Miami. They appeared to be interested in me, especially about living in Miami. Then out of nowhere, through perhaps some drug-induced clairvoyance, the seductress asked me point blank, "Are you married?"

I was taken aback, so I laughed somewhat nervously to buy myself time. I didn't want to lie, so I responded with a question and an inflection that the notion was ridiculous, "Why would you think that?"

She looked at me with penetrating, fuck-me eyes and took a final drag off her self-rolled cigarette before tapping it out in an ashtray as she blew smoke into the air. Then shrugging her shoulders she said matter-of-factly, "You seem like you might be married." Luckily her friend changed the subject before I had to answer.

Our conversation was soon drowned out by three girls at another table, a blonde, a brunette, and a redhead. They were having an increasingly animated discussion in German. It appeared to be about someone's boyfriend. They got so loud that the nice girl at our table offered her own opinion on the situation, causing the three girls to laugh hysterically. Before I knew it, the other girls joined our table.

So there I was sitting with five girls who were all about twenty years old. *Just when it seemed the trip couldn't get any crazier*, I thought to myself. And for a brief moment, I felt like a king.

Everyone made introductions, and the girls all friended each other on Facebook. I thought that was weird since as far as I could tell they had just met, but Europeans fucking love Facebook. Most of my friends from home hate it. Maybe it goes back to that whole European openness thing.

Anyway, I sat there feeling somewhat out of place as I tried to follow the continuation of the girl's story, which was all in German. Apparently it involved some guy the redhead was dating who was either really bad in bed or really good, I couldn't tell which. All five of the girls were talking a mile a minute, and the nice Turkish girl noticed I was left out, so she tried to add me to the conversation, "Allan is from Miami."

The three new girls seemed impressed, and the blonde started asking me all these questions, "Oh, Miami. *Miami Vice*," she said through a thick German accent. I laughed, trying to give her my best smile and feeling cool at being from a famous city.

The girl continued with the joke. "Tell me, Mr. Miami Vice, are you a cop?"

"No." I shook my head with a courtesy laugh.

"I don't believe you," she said, taking a drag off her cigarette. "You look like a cop to me." All the girls laughed.

"I'm not a cop," I promised.

Then she went into this big soliloquy, "I love America; America is so cool; English is my favorite subject in school; I just love doing my English lessons and learning about America." At first I thought she might be coming on to me, but then she kept exaggerating every word in a way that I couldn't tell if she was being sincere or if her English was just really bad.

She continued in this exaggerated tone, "English is so awesome; America is so awesome." I knew from past experience that Europeans often make fun of Americans for overusing the word "awesome." I was shocked; I hadn't used the word; I was just trying to make conversation with people from another culture, and here I was being made fun of right to my face as she droned on in her ditziest voice, "I love traveling around Europe; Europe is so awesome."

Suddenly her heavy accent went away, and she spoke perfect English. "Tell me, Mr. Policeman, do you speak German?"

By now my partial smile had been replaced with a stone face. "Not really," I said, "I know a few words, like *danke*."

"Why don't you speak German?" she asked like an interrogator. "You're in Germany." I shrugged my shoulders, too surprised to think of a response.

She wouldn't let up. "Here, I'll teach you some German. Repeat after me." She said a phrase, and her friends laughed. I assumed it was a curse word or maybe even an insult towards myself. I didn't repeat it. I sat there silent. "Repeat, Mr. Policeman. Repeat. You're in Germany; you have to learn some German," she said as if I was a stupid preschooler. I didn't say anything.

"Okay," she went on, "if you ever want to talk to a girl in Germany, here's what you say." Again she said a phrase I couldn't understand, and most of the girls laughed. I knew she was making fun of me, and I wasn't going to give her the satisfaction, so I just sat there waiting for her to be finished. I could tell the nice Turkish girl was getting uncomfortable with the situation.

I felt like I had been nothing but nice and respectful. I've never had someone be so mean to me when I had done so little. In fact it was for nothing other than where I was from. And the whole time I was so caught off guard I couldn't think of anything to say.

The thing is, she was really pretty. She would have been a poster girl in Hitler's Germany with her blonde hair, blue eyes, and perfect cheekbones. Although her ginger friend may not have done well and neither would the Turkish girl.

It was odd to see someone so pretty have so much anger and hate. It made me wonder what had happened in her past to make her feel that way. Maybe some American guy had screwed her over at some point.

After several more insults, the blonde finally left. The remaining four girls started a new conversation in German until the Turkish girl said, "Okay, let's speak English so everyone can talk." The other girls looked at her for a moment. "We should give a good impression of Berlin," she explained, and they acquiesced.

It was a very nice gesture, but unfortunately the damage had already been done. And once I got over the initial shellshock, I reverted to a vitriolic jingoism that would haunt me the rest of the trip.

{138}

Berlin is amazing, but I kind of want to blow it up. There's an underlying hipster arrogance, which is the worst kind. The city is becoming a San Francisco, obsessively smelling its own flatulence and thinking it doesn't stink.

Yesterday I endured mocking condescension from an Eva Braun–type bitch. I wish I had been more prepared for it. I wish I had said something, but it was so hateful, so unexpected. There was deep anger there somewhere.

I am sorry for your freedom, Eva. Fuck you and your cultural insecurities. Your language is dead, and you know it. You and your perfect English know it.

Half of Berlin will die of lung cancer. That will be the new hipster thing to do.

I feel like Maynard, wanting a geographical area to fall into the ocean or be swallowed into the ground, but instead of California, it's Berlin.

I am monolingual.

"Asphyxia"

Fall—
Into the sea.
Drown—
Below the air.
Struggle—
To survive.
Until—
You have died.

{139}

Why do I focus on the rude person and hate the whole country based on her? Why don't I focus on the nice person who explicitly said she wanted to give a good impression of Berlin?

"Anti-asphyxia"

Head
onto the road,
Live
life bold,
Learn
for your brain,
Sing
for your soul,
Breath
for your lungs,
Dance
for your passion.

{140}

Here I sit with my pen and my coffee. Berlin lovers walk past me holding hands. Have I become a writer? Is it now who I am? Am I finally unafraid?

What have I learned from this trip? Anything? Nothing?

Are you fuckin' retarded, or are you a fuckin' cocksucker? Why am I so angry? Why are other people so unaware of themselves, making fucking constant noise? Is their self-absorbance beautiful or obnoxious?

I think I'm the only clean-shaven guy in all Berlin.

I suspect that at least two of the girls from last night were high. One probably coke, the other maybe MDMA.

When I go home, then what? It's time to publish. Time to finish products. To make songs.

My Current Projects:
1. *The Twelve Days of Summer*
2. Songs with the Manner Born
3. *Random Thoughts and Broken Lines* or whatever this is
4. *The Czech Cowboy*
5. Justin and Allan's story

Potential Trips Abroad:
1. Amsterdam with Shelly
2. France
3. Solo Portugal
4. Southeastern Europe
5. Asia

"Let's make party." Everyone says the Germans in Berlin speak perfect English, but compared to the Finns and the Swedes, the Germans are fucking retarded.

"When the Bombs Fell"

When the bombs fell,
did you run for cover?
When the bombs fell,
did you cry for your mother?
When the bombs fell,
did you regret
that you started it?
When the bombs fell,
did you think of the bombs you dropped,
and what those people thought?
When the bombs fell,
were you surprised,
your superiority unrealized?
When the bombs fell,
did you want to die,
cry
lie
down and wait for it to be over,
Or go out and fight?
Was there anyone left to fight?

Every day you live free
Every day you cross a border
Every day you live without poverty
and misery
with your giant GDP,
you can thank us.

Every day you call yourself German,
and speak your language,
you can thank us.

{141}

The world should forever keep nukes aimed down the throat of Germany. They've earned that right.

Will Germans ever be able to separate themselves from evil? No, and they don't deserve to.

You can thank us for McDonald's, Coca-Cola, Facebook, Google, Apple, your movies, songs, and a language that doesn't sound like someone raping a rat with a sandpaper condom.

That blonde girl's issue is probably insecurity at her own national irrelevance. Or maybe some American fucked her over in the past; she was pretty cute after all. Whatever the reason, she didn't have to take it out on me. All I ask is that I warrant my criticisms.

"Goose Steps"

Steel boots on cobblestone,
seeking emperor approval
under the Tor.
A Brandenburg agenda
for world domination.

{142}

Fuck cell phones and the people who talk on them loudly.

I'll probably never go to Dunkin' Donuts again if I can help it. Starbucks is way better, but apparently in Germany they don't sell the Americano even though they had it in Prague. Interesting.

Fuck all nonfunctional scarves, you faggoty-ass hipsters.

"Permeation"

Psst, other countries,
You've been invaded and don't even know it;
Your old squares are full of our stores,
Your TVs are full of our shows, theaters full of our movies,
and radios full of our songs.

{143}

<u>Things I've learned on this trip:</u>

I'm more American than I thought, and I have a ton of nationalistic pride, bordering on outright jingoism.

I'm not going back peaceful. I've felt angry and annoyed a lot the last few days. I just can't seem to escape people, and everyone has such little self-awareness.

I've started writing a lot. It seems the road stimulates my mind and ideas.

Although I'm not going home in a tranquil mood, I am going back motivated. Motivated to make it as a writer, to finish my projects. Writing will allow me to live the exact type of life I want. It is also a good outlet, especially as my emotions get more extreme.

Joy Division (recommended band).

That German girl left a bad taste in my mouth. She still makes me really angry. Hopefully something redeems Europe and my trip doesn't end with that experience.

I've only been told to shut up by a stranger twice in my life. And both times were by an Irish person in Europe. I'm definitely ready to go home.

I think I got what I came for from Berlin, although the warm beaches of Croatia probably would have been nicer.

I've formed a lot of opinions about different nationalities, mostly negative. I've also learned to appreciate my own even more.

Do Germans instinctively march in time? Assholes.

I'm energized and excited to see Shelly.

My goals for the trip are complete. It has been a fascinating journey and has exceeded my expectations.

I need to finish more songs for the Manner Born.

I need to finish *The Twelve Days of Summer*. That is my biggest priority.

My wanderlust should be satisfied for a little while.

I'm not gonna miss paying to use the bathroom.

It will be nice to speak in colloquialisms.

When I get home, it will be fall and the middle of football season. Oh, and all the fucking political drama of the presidential primary. I wonder what's happening with my grandmother's will—geez. Not much to gain, plenty to lose.

It seems people are more curious about you when you're traveling alone.

I'm not sure what to do about work. I've been offered about fifty doc review jobs since I've been gone.

I love having my whereabouts unknown, being unreachable, anonymous.

No matter where I am, there are always dogs barking. Bullet silences the barking dog.

Will I ever get sick of *High Violet*? It has been my savior this whole trip, my savior from snoring and annoying people.

When I came back from Maui I was tranquil. I'm not tranquil after this.

If I look five years younger than I am, then theoretically I have five more years of traveling this way. So it shouldn't be unreasonable to try and get two more years.

I'm tired and in need of exercise and alcohol detox.

On my trip to Ireland, Michael Jackson died. On this trip, Steve Jobs died.

I need to memorize the order of all the places I've visited. I've been doing about one big trip a year. Next year might be more. I travel to sow oats, to know I'm not dead, to gain self-confidence, to write, and to dance.

I used to run and lift weights.

My hamstring should be healed by now. I look forward to playing basketball again.

I fell asleep in the Tiergarten for the second time in my life; the first time was three years ago.

Maybe I've made a new friend this trip in Mark. That's always a goal—a friend that I stay in touch with, to have one friend from each epoch of my life.

In the modern age, maybe there are no more San Franciscos. Maybe with the Internet, it's wherever you are.

"As My Pen Gently Writes"

The sun settles over the trees,
shining through the leaves.
The wind blows,
sprinkling soft grass
with signs of autumn.
And an occasional chill runs through my skin,
as I gently move my pen.

The best part of the road is that if you don't like where you are or who you're with, you can just leave, e.g., the neo-Nazi racist mick.

The beautiful park is littered with old candy wrappers, bottle caps, and other trash not thrown away.

German denigration—was that girl making fun of me or Europeans who like Americans? Either way it was weird.

I'm attracted to the mad ones.

"The Mad Ones"

I'm attracted to the mad ones.
Tattoos on necks,
reckless wandering hearts
acting on impulse.
Heavy drinking
Drowning demons,
I can understand.
The kindred spirits of the road,
running from
and searching for
something,
all at the same time.

I go home knowing what I need to do. It's only since April or May of this year that I've fully embraced my creative roots. I have two years to live however I want, to try and make it. Really I have the rest of my life, but I'll try it this way for now.

I need to finish my artistic projects. I'll talk to Shelly about what to do regarding work.

Can I finish *Twelve Days* by December 1st?

As far as making music with my neighbor, I feel like we just need to set aside the time and get it done. Maybe we'll come to Berlin to explore ideas.

I love that no one knows where I am right now, and I am completely unreachable.

Shelly and I can finally start studying French. We should make a list of things to do that might help us learn, such as putting our phones in French and finding out about events at the French embassy.

I just want to write, create, and take trips. Maybe I'll visit Europe with other friends.

I like people who are interested in me but not necessarily in total awe like the girl from Estonia.

I need to spend some time with my folks again soon, especially my dad. Life is precious, and they're getting old.

I like this notebook size and style. It's not as nice as the hipster notebooks though. Fuck them, the hipsters I mean.

I should write a song about hipsters, just write down a bunch of attributes about them.

Have I changed? Will I be different after this? Better?

Tara said I was the same, and I feel like she must not have known me very well before, or she doesn't know me now.

There are incredibly beautiful women in Helsinki and Tallinn.

I wonder how that blonde girl's ginger friend would have fared in Nazi Germany.

It's crazy how people from the Leipzig seminar have stayed in touch. At least five of us are living in DC. I knew them way less than anyone else from school, and yet I'm in touch with them way more. I guess it's a pretty specific group, a subsample of a sample.

Perhaps the Leipzig trip changed my life, made me realize how much fun I have traveling abroad.

It's the job of the poet to explore aspects of the human condition and relate them in a way that elicits emotion or thought so that others can better experience the human condition.

"Travelers"

Across the ocean
Across your dreams
Across the world
as it all seems.
Heroes walk in valleys
and on mountains,
reaching for the stars.
While others drown in bars
suffocating to pay off cars,
the heroes run with packs,
all possessions on their backs.

{144}

I curse Justin for taking one of my long-sleeved shirts as I shiver in front of the Bundestag.

"Landmarks"

The Brandenburg Gate
and six million sent to a horrific fate
The Reichstag
and the death squad
Berlin
and unspeakable sin
The Tiger tank
and Anne Frank
Mercedes
and killing babies
The trains
and all their pains,
cattle cars for people.
How were you ever allowed to survive?
I suppose but what,
let the Soviets have you and all your resources?
There should have been a Fat Man for you,
to show you how it feels,
melting skin
in Berlin
radiation
deformation,
a taste of your own abomination.

{145}

So tired.

I was woken up early this morning by some asshole Chileans. Fuck them. The fucking assholes couldn't be bothered to pack the night before. Shouldn't they be trapped in a copper mine somewhere?

Then later in the day, my nap in the Tiergarten was interrupted by a barking dog.

I'm tired, and my reflection is done. I want to go home.

EPILOGUE

"And just like that, it's over—you're home."

{1}

As I waited for my flight out of Zurich, I had some more time to reflect on the trip.

Another goal accomplished, the great European backpacking tour. Doing the whole Eurail thing. I always wanted to know what that was like, and it's pretty incredible.

Traveling like this with no agenda, no itinerary, just going wherever the road takes us creates so many highs and lows, ups and downs. There are moments of total elation followed by times of near depression. It's amazing—the cities, the people, the memories.

In Amsterdam, I met a girl who said she was studying to be an informatica. What's an informatica?

On the Baltic Sea, we drank a bottle of Salmiakki.

In Berlin, I met a girl who said she couldn't travel any longer because she was running out of money, then I watched her buy forty euros worth of drinks in about two hours.

If you finger a girl who is on her period, can you get AIDS through blood on a hangnail?

Berlin is cool except for the Germans. Germans can try to be attractive and socially advanced, but in the end they are still Germans. *Your language exists because of our good graces, you Deutsch cunt. Go fuck yourself, Eva.*

I'm pretty sure that by most any objective standard I am a horrible person.

A pretty girl walks past me in the airport, and I want to bathe her in semen.

I wish I could have one night where I could sleep without someone waking me up with a bunch of stupid fucking noise. My god, the train ride to Zurich was terrible. They added someone to our cabin in the middle of the night. And the walls between the rooms were paper-thin and actually seemed to amplify any noise from next door.

In Krakow, I met my first asshole of the trip, an Irishman. The Poles themselves seemed okay even if some of them were a little standoffish. Unfortunately I didn't have enough interaction with them to make a clear judgment.

The only Europeans I've truly liked so far in my travels have been the Finns and the Spanish. I used to like the Irish, but now I'm not sure. Danes seem okay. The verdict is still out on the Poles. Swedes I'm indifferent. Not sure about the Dutch. Estonians seem okay. Russians make me uneasy. I generally dislike Germans and people from Prague. And of course I've long had a low opinion of Italians.

Typically I come back from a trip with more admiration for people, but I think I generally dislike Europeans. I've never been prouder to be American nor happier to be going home after a trip abroad.

Other countries don't think outside the box like Americans do. I wonder if it's because they've killed so many of their dreamers over the centuries and the few that were left went to America.

The truth is that as much as I love traveling, I often hate most other travelers or at least the backpackers in the tourist areas. It's also surprising how many cities I dislike.

I still want to take Shelly to Amsterdam. I would also like to go to Portugal based on Mark's recommendation. I'm wary of going to France because I fear rudeness. I want to learn French because it's beautiful, not because I like the people.

Naturally I'm sad to see this trip ending, but I'm excited to see my friends, to play ball, to make music, to laugh and just hang out. It will also be nice to finally have good, dependable Wi-Fi, some peace and quiet, and people I can understand. Oh my god, and having my own bathroom will be amazing.

{2}

I've never had a permanent legal job. Rather I get hired temporarily to work on corporate litigation or antitrust cases. It's just something I do, not who I am. Then who am I? A traveler?

EPILOGUE

While waiting for my flight, I went to the bathroom to shave. Men in suits streamed in and out of the restroom hurrying to catch their planes. Almost certainly some of them were attorneys, the life I could've had. Instead, my back hurt, I'd been wearing the same pants for five days, and I was nearly out of money. And yet, I wouldn't have traded places with them for anything.

{3}

Much of what I do is so I can say I did it when I could. So that when I look back years from now, I will have no regrets about not taking a chance. In a way, I am constantly preparing for my deathbed so that when I reflect on my life I feel satisfied.

Sometimes I think I may not have much time left. Either I'm becoming more mad or no longer running from the madness. Or maybe, hopefully, I'm just really tired.

The Irishman, that German girl, I want to hunt them down and kill them, not just them but their whole families, their whole societies. I did nothing to them, and yet they verbally attacked me. I held no malice towards them, and yet they brought malice towards me.

But I know what I have to do. It's the only thing I can do. I have to write. I have to try and channel these emotions into art because nothing makes me angrier than being unfairly criticized or maligned. All I ask is that my criticisms be fair.

When I get home, I have to be very careful. I need Shelly to watch my behavior in case it deteriorates to the point of requiring medication. I just hope there will be clear warning signs first.

"Portents"

As my stability begins to wane,
I wonder,
how long will I stay sane.

{4}

I've finally made it on the plane, and some screaming kid is making it impossible to read. Goddammit, there is no sanctuary.

And now I'm somewhere over the mid-Atlantic drinking shit coffee, and I mean absolute shit.

One of the last things Mark said to me was: "I'll be your writing community." And then he challenged me to write a short story about the Czech Cowboy.

I generally don't feel guilt, not because I'm a psychopath, but because I don't think it's logical. I think guilt is a wasted emotion. If something makes me feel guilty, then instead of spending time worrying about it, I modify my future behavior to avoid that feeling.

After the blonde left the table in Berlin, I asked her friends why she hated Americans. Everyone became uncomfortable and one of the girls muttered something about her just being really sarcastic, but that only seemed like an ad hoc attempt to diffuse the situation.

Interestingly, I think I could learn German pretty quickly. Both times I've been to Germany, I seemed to get it somehow.

I wish I could give Shelly more. Her grace and patience astound me. It's also strange how I'm becoming friends with her brother, communicating independently via email.

The line on the bridge of my nose is getting deeper, the only physical tell of my true age. Well, that and my fast-growing mustache. I swear, half my life is spent on hair removal.

With all the ups and downs of this trip, of this type of travel, I've learned that when you can't control your environment, you have to adapt to it. I've also learned that I'm very attracted to girls with tattoos—tattoos and madness. Of course the two often go hand in hand. I've always been drawn to the mad ones—Morrison, Lennon, Cohen—always. I used to not pay attention to it. I used to think it was merely infatuation, but now I think it's who I am.

Maybe I'll get les États-Unis tattooed on my right forearm, a representation of my two sides: in my heart is a traveler, but in my veins is America.

"The Madness Express"

Clouds of grandeur
Virginary visions
Dreams of competence
Victorious hopes
Einsteigen bitte

{5}

The clouds look like ski slopes as we descend into Dulles. Myriad memories run through my mind, and I wonder if they actually happened.

"I think I am able to suppress these feelings," Mari had said after I told her the truth. Apparently she was mistaken.

I hope my grandmother had a nice funeral.

That German girl clearly had some national image issues. The Irish clearly need a lesson in manners taught by a fist to the jaw. Maybe that's a language they can understand given their mouth-full-of-shit accent.

We're at 15,000 feet and have traveled 4,070 miles.

I let out a sigh for all the women I will never have.

"Mein Descent"

Drink a goblet of desire,
with loins on fire.
At the bar,
searching for whoever you are.
It doesn't really matter,
whether you're slim or fatter.
I need to be in someone,
forget tomorrow,
and have fun.
I'll beg or borrow,
to get what I need,
for the craving I must feed.

{6}

And just like that, it's over—you're home. The cities, the trains, the foreign voices all fade away in the tranquility of your own bedroom.

No more waking up to zipping suitcases. No more showers with sandals. No more ordering food off a menu you can't understand. No more spontaneity. The drinking, well, the drinking continues for the most part.

I am home, and I am glad to be home, yet my next trip is not far from my mind. Who knows what it will be? Belgium, Luxembourg, Amsterdam with my wife, Portugal on my own, Asia, France?

I have an odd sense of tranquility. A certain calm to not get too worked up. It's unexpected given how angry I was when I left. I'm glad to have it though.

You can't take a trip like that and not have it change you. Something must come of it—peacefulness, a renewed commitment to write, satisfaction at embracing youth when you could—something.

"Sweet Memoriam"

Blemishless skin,
The voice I will never hear again,
Meeting for wine
That became your place or mine,
Eyes that are oceans deep
That I will only ever see in my sleep.

EPILOGUE

{7}

I am happy, content. There are things that I should do, that I need to do, but I want to enjoy these feelings of tranquility while I can. I want to decompress before I return to the grind.

I've started typing up my notebooks. I'm really glad I kept a journal. After all, you don't miss what you can't remember.

It's nice to be able to use a computer, my own computer with my own settings. All the material comforts of home make it feel like the obstacles of the road never even happened. Is the road real—not working, bouncing from town to town, fleeting interactions with strangers? Maybe it's only real for that time, for that moment.

Gradually it will happen: you check something online, then you're looking at new products and then news and soon you're right back into the rat race—no more journaling, no more thinking. Life becomes less about experience and more about being part of the machine.

Somehow you have to make the machine work for you. Use the Wi-Fi, but don't let it own you. Get what you need and get out. It's all about balance.

I am desperately trying to stay in a tranquil place. I have to write. Like a quadriplegic stranded on a beach with a rising tide, I am completely naked without my pen.

I have to keep my mind and my heart where they were on the trip. Thus, I have to be very careful with my decision making. My life, right now, is mine.

Now is the time for final products. That's what I'm home for, to write, to work on relationships, and to finish my projects.

This is where it gets good—the mountains start to shake, and the river begins to shift.

{8}
"Wilting Rose"

Our love becomes
a wilting rose.
Slowly, the color fades.
Imperceptible at first,
talk less often,
important dates forgotten.
Then noticeable,
petals curling over
laughter gone
intimacy disappearing.
Give it light
Give it water
But it's too late,
not enough.
A petal falls,
heart grows heavy,
like watching your own funeral.
Sit in silence,
wishing for something,
a CPR for love.
Another petal drops,
divided possessions

and memories,
shared past lost forever.

What if you could go back,
Before the pressures of time and life,
to that brilliant glow,
when everything seemed so . . .
perfect.
Mark the moment
Stop the fading
But you cannot prevent
the degrading,
of a rose.

{9}

"Wilted Rose"

A wilting rose,
the color fades
until, a petal drops,
then another,
until, there's just a stem
. . . with thorns.

www.ingramcontent.com/pod-product-compliance
Lightning Source LLC
Chambersburg PA
CBHW031347040426
42444CB00005B/217